WORLD

by Demetrio Sodi Morales
Drawings by Alberto Beltrán

Chaac,
Rain God

They knew how to count time,
even within themselves.
The moon, the wind, the year, the day,
they all move, but also pass on.
All blood reaches its place of rest,
as all power reaches its throne...
Chilam Balam of Chumayel

TITLES IN THE MINUTIAE MEXICANA SERIES

A Guide to Mexico's Butterflies and Moths
A Bird Watcher's Guide to Mexico
A Guide to Mexican Mammals and Reptiles
A Flower Lover's Guide to Mexico
A Guide to Mexican Archaeology
A Guide to Mexican History
A Guide to Mexican Witchcraft
A Guide to Tequila, Mezcal and Pulque
A Guide to Mexican Poetry, Ancient and Modern
A Guide to Architecture in Ancient Mexico
Minute Guide to Speaking Spanish
Recipes and Memories of Mexico
The Cross in Mexico
For the Love of Mexico
A Guide to Mexican Ceramics
Oaxaca, Crafts and Sightseeing
Oaxaca, The Archaeological Record
The Maya World
The Aztecs Then and Now
The Great Temple and the Aztec Gods

Fourth edition, December, 1997

ISBN 968-7074-41-8 (cuarta edición revisada y corregida)
ISBN 968-7074-25-6

Editorial MINUTIAE MEXICANA, S. A de C.V.
Insurgentes Centro 114-207, 06030, México, D. F.

There are many representations of Quetzalcoatl, a god ancient in Middle America before the Christian era began. We have adopted as the insignia of our series the most common — that of the feathered serpent. The father and creator of man, Quetzalcoatl was the beneficent god of life and the wind, the god of civilization who inspired man to study the stars, to develop agriculture, industry and the arts.

Impreso y hecho en México

TABLE OF CONTENTS

PROLOGUE 5

MAYA TERRITORY 7
The southern or highland zone, 7; The central or lowland zone, 8; Map, 9; Northern zone, 10

MAYA LANGUAGES 12
The Huastec enigma, 14

WHAT HAPPENED TO THE ANCIENT MAYA 16

THE LACANDON 19
The Chol Lacandón, 21; The Yucatec Lacandón, 22; The Naha Lacandón, 23; Ancient gods and rites persist, 24

TRAVELING INTO THE MAYA AREA 29
Comalcalco, 29; Villahermosa, 30; Palenque, 31; The royal tomb, 33

CAMPECHE AND THE CONSERVATIVE MAYA 40
The conservative Maya, 42; Kinship, 43; Company and cross, 44; Godparents and baptism, 44; Deities, old and new, 45; Home and hearth, 48; Going modern, 50

MERIDA, MONUMENTS AND MARVELOUS FOOD IN YUCATAN 51
Uxmal, 54; Dzibilchaltún, 56; Mayapán, 57; Chichén Itzá, 59

WAR OF CASTES 65
Talking idols, 66; The Tzotzil war, 71; During Holy Week, 75; Carnival festivities, 75

THE ANCIENT MAYA 77
The proto-Maya, 78; The mother culture, 79; Historical periods, 80; Theory to explain collapse, 83; Chichén and the Itzá, 86; War and decline, 88

MATHEMATICS AND THE CALENDAR SYSTEM 90
Solar and ritual calendars, 90; Numbers and systems, 94; Counting of time, 96; The starting date, 98; Recording of dates, 99

MAYA LITERATURE AND THEATER 102
Maya hieroglyphs, 104; Writings, 107; Maya theater, 115

PROPHECIES OF THE CONQUEST 126
Came the conquerors, 128

EPILOGUE 130

SOURCES FOR STUDYING THE MAYA 132

REVISIONS since 1987: Wendy Schonfeld, Precolumbian and Primitive Art historian and archaeologist, studying for her doctorate at Columbia. University.

COVER: Carved figures from a lintel at Yaxchilán, against a background of "Maya blue," a color that was applied to pottery figurines, vases, and used in mural paintings, and identifies the work as pre-Hispanic Maya.

The Palace at Palenque is a building unique in Maya architecture. It has the only four-story tower yet found in Mesoamerica. Although the Palace, which measures 300 ft. by 240 ft., may have been a residence — given the presence of drains — the tower would have provided a strategic view of the surrounding area. The presence of a Venus glyph in the tower may also indicate its use as an astronomical observatory. The Palace is decorated with stucco relief carvings in its rooms and galleries which are grouped around open patios. The presence of human figures in one relief each with an arm raised to the opposite shoulder (a gesture of submission) may indicate that the Palace was also an administrative center or center for state ritual. *Photo Doris Heyden.*

PROLOGUE

Maya ruins tell us that the people who built the once magnificent cities possessed an incredible culture, unique, and superior in some respects to those of other Mesoamerican civilizations.

Imagining Maya cities as they must have been in all their splendor, it is not difficult to understand how their creators managed to perfect such intellectual achievements as an exact calendar, and the use of a complex writing system that is still in the process of being deciphered.

All this suggests a disciplined social behavior, functional socio-economic structures, and an equilibrium of spiritual values that the Maya surely had first to develop.

But as in all human affairs, among the Maya there were fluctuations that finally brought them to a decline from which they probably never would have recovered. It was this state of affairs that prevailed when the Spanish conquerors made contact with them in 1511, when one of Spanish explorer Valdivia's ships was wrecked off the east coast of the Yucatán Peninsula during an expedition from Panama to Santo Domingo. But at the time, the Spaniards were unable to recognize that decline for what it was, inasmuch as they knew nothing of Maya history.

Two Spanish survivors of the shipwreck became the first Europeans to penetrate the mysteries of Maya culture as they found it, still free from all contact with the West. Their names were Jerónimo de Aguilar and Gonzalo Guerrero. Both were to play important roles with respect to their fellow Spaniards. Guerrero, integrated into the Maya culture, married, and with two children born on the Peninsula, fought on the side of the Maya against the conquerors. Aguilar, a lay brother forced into slavery by his captors, joined Hernán Cortés at Cozumel in 1519 and continued on with him, serving as his interpreter during the conquest of the Aztec Empire.

The Peninsula of Yucatán was discovered for the western world by Francisco Hernández de Córdoba in 1517. Many years were to pass, however, before anyone concerned himself with the systematic collection of data on the culture of the Maya in the 16th century.

That pioneer was Fray Diego de Landa, third Bishop of Yucatán, who arrived on the Peninsula in 1549 when the Maya culture, though on the wane, was still in evidence. Landa embodied all the contradictions peculiar to educated men of that period, who had absorbed many Renaissance ideas but without overcoming completely the limitations of the medieval mentality. On one hand, during autos-de-fé and in truly fanatical acts, Landa destroyed cultural remains, burned codices, and sat in inquisitorial judgment on numerous Indians stubbornly opposed to abandoning their ancient traditions. At the same time, he carefully collected the data he regarded as most significant, relative to the culture he was helping to destroy. In 1566, during a stay in Spain, he compiled the information he had been gathering since 1549 into the most important source material we have on the Maya culture: *Relación de las Cosas de Yucatán* (Report on the Things of Yucatán).

It is with Landa, then, that the study of the Maya begins, notably intensified and enriched during the past 100 years.

MAYA TERRITORY

The Maya occupied a territory of some 117,000 square miles, an area as immense as it is varied in climate and topography. That variation in physical environment undoubtedly influenced local cultural manifestations; hence the diversity of artistic styles evident as one traverses the territory. Yet all that wealth of expression preserves an impressive unity.

In general terms, the region occupied by the ancient Maya is that now included within the boundaries of the Mexican states of Yucatán, Campeche, Tabasco, Quintana Roo and the eastern half of Chiapas; the greater part of Guatemala, excepting only a strip along the Pacific Coast; the western section of Honduras, a smaller portion of El Salvador, and Belize or British Honduras.

Today, Maya occupation is limited to small but numerous communities scattered throughout the vast territory in which their astounding ancestors created high culture.

The territory can be divided into three geographical zones. One is composed of mountain chains and intermediate tablelands, the Cordillera of Central America, that forms a half circle towards the southwest, south and southeast. Another has as its center the interior basin of the Department of El Petén in Guatemala, stretching east to the Caribbean, northwest to the Gulf of Mexico, and including the southern section of the Yucatán Peninsula. The third is the northern zone of Yucatán—flat limestone lowlands, covered with shrubs and underbrush, but rich in cultural remains.

THE SOUTHERN OR HIGHLAND ZONE

In this zone the mountains reach an altitude of more than 13,200 feet, and the majority are of volcanic origin. These high peaks are in Guatemala; the highlands that stretch into Chiapas are dotted with lower peaks, around 3,500 feet. The rainy season is generally from May to November; winters are dry and cold with frost in the high mountains, and summers are cooler than in the other two zones.

The highland lakes—Amatitlán, Atitlán, Izabal—are of singular beauty; the land is rich in mammals, reptiles and birds. The gorgeous quetzal bird, so important to the ancient Maya as a symbolic element in their religion, lives almost exclusively in the highlands of Guatemala, Honduras and Chiapas.

For a long time it was thought that corn might have originated in this zone, but recent explorations appear to indicate that it was developed farther north on Mexico's central plateau. Still feasible, however, is the hypothesis that the Maya may have initiated their own agricultural systems in the western highlands of Guatemala.

THE CENTRAL OR LOWLAND ZONE

The second Maya territorial zone ranges from 500 to 1,000 feet above sea level in the central savanna of El Petén; but in the middle of the Lacandón jungle there are elevations of up to 4,000 feet. It is a moving experience to climb slowly up these hills and observe the change from tropical to highland vegetation. One such ascent terminates at a beautiful lagoon, aptly named Ocotal Grande (Great Pine Grove).

Two river systems cross the Central Region, one formed by the Motagua river that rises in the Department of Quiché, Guatemala, and empties into the Gulf of Honduras. The second system is that of the Usumacinta and its three main tributaries: the Pasión, the

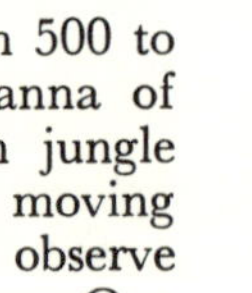

NORTHERN ZONE

CENTRAL OR LOWLAND ZONE

SOUTHERN ZONE

PUTUN TRANSPENINSULAR ROUTE

THE MAYA AREA

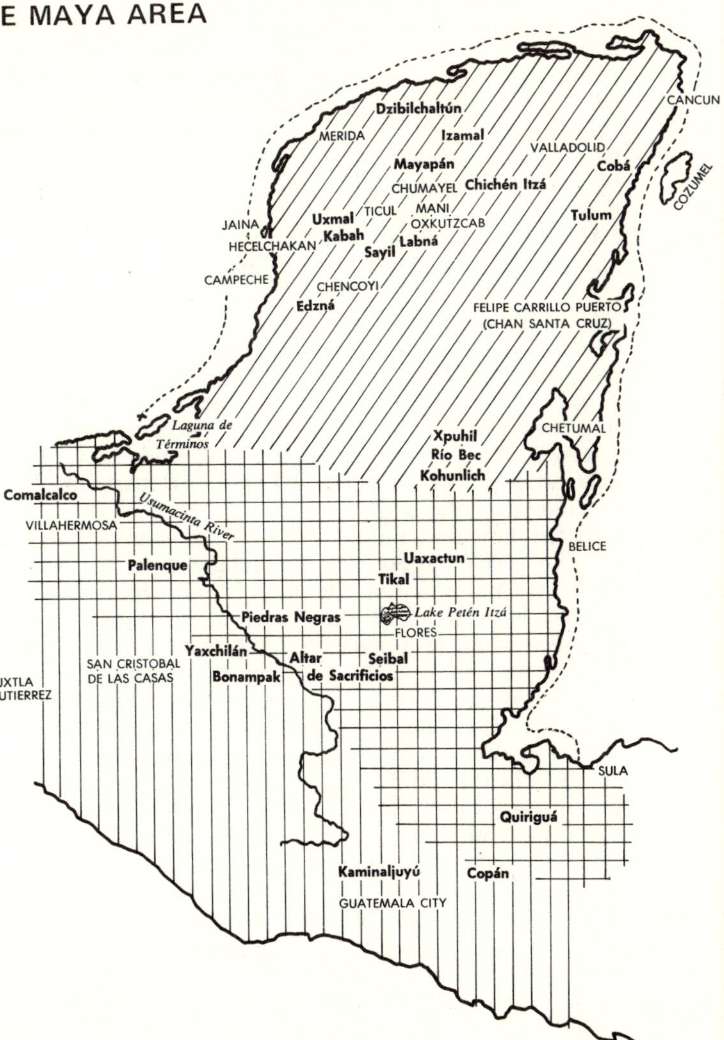

Chixoy, and the Lacantún. Both the Pasión and the Chixoy rise in Guatemala, and at the point of their confluence is the site of an ancient Maya city called Altar de Sacrificios. The Lacantún joins the Pasión and Chixoy 20 miles beyond Altar de Sacrificios to become the splendid and spectacular Usumacinta, the River of the Sacred Monkey, that finally empties into the Gulf of Mexico.

Hills and valleys are covered with lush tropical vegetation sheltering abundant wildlife, both now threatened with extinction due to thoughtless exploitation.

Here the climate is extremely hot and humid. It rains almost the year round although, theoretically, the rainy season is from May to January. Limestone deposits are plentiful in the region and, together with wood and lime, provided the three elements necessary for construction. As a result, in this zone we find some of the most beautiful Maya cities: Palenque, Bonampak, Piedras Negras, Yaxchilán.

In the northern part of El Petén savanna there are 14 lakes. The largest is Petén Itzá, known to the ancients as Chaltuná. On one of its islands stood Tayasal, the last stronghold of the Maya, where they fortified themselves and retained their culture until 1697, when the city was finally subjugated by the Spaniards.

Between the savanna and the northern limits of the zone there is a chain of hills that appears to look sadly upon the few streams that cut through it. Trees are sparse, and the land does not lend itself to the cultivation of corn, although it provides good pasture. These conditions probably account for the almost total absence of remains of ancient dwellings.

THE NORTHERN ZONE

The third geographic zone of Maya territory, the northern half of the Yucatán Peninsula, is covered by low, dense thornbush. An arm of the highland jungle extends well into the northeastern section of the Peninsula, with cedar, mahogany, zapote, and other precious, hardwood trees. On all sides are areas where the vegetation gives way to large expanses of limestone soil, this zone being extremely arid, almost without lakes, and with rivers that are mere brooks. Even the mountains shrink here. In this immense horizontal extension there is only one chain of low hills that begins at Champotón on the west coast of the Peninsula. This area is known as *puuc* (hilly country) in the Maya language of Yucatán.

Natural wells, called *cenotes* (from the Maya *dzonoot)* are practically the sole source of water on the Peninsula, and are formed by the caving in of the limestone soil to reveal subterranean pools. They may be as large as 200 feet in diameter and hundreds of feet deep. One of the most famous is that of Chichén Itzá where offerings, human and otherwise, were made to the water deities. The tale told to visitors today is that the victims were maidens thrown into the cenote to assuage the rain god Chaac who lived in its depths. The skeletal remains that have been recovered by modern subaquatic exploration, however, indicate that both sexes were sacrificed and that some were children. (Children were favorites of the water gods, above all those who shed many tears.) Supposedly, a victim who remained alive until sunset was rescued to deliver any message from Chaac. The cenote depths have also yielded up offerings in gold, rubber, wood, and jade.

The Maya invented another technique to collect the scarce rain water. They constructed *chultunes,* or cisterns, a kind of subterranean bottle lined with stone, into which rain water drained. Often the surface area around the mouth was paved to keep the water clean. Even today, chultunes can be found in some Maya communities, the opening covered by great stone slabs to prevent contamination of the priceless liquid.

The pheasant and the deer have always been characteristic of this zone. In their sonorous tongue, the Yucatec Maya describe the territory as *u luumil cutz, u luumil ceh, mayab u kabah,* "it is the land of the pheasant, the land of the deer, and Mayab is its name."

MAYA LANGUAGES

Since 1884 when Otto Stoll first undertook to classify the Maya languages by comparing the vocabularies to which he had access, other attempts have been made. The classification most widely accepted at present is that of Norman A. McQuown.

Maya culture has expressed itself through many tongues and while all, of course, belong to the same linguistic trunk, Maya, in some cases they are so different that people living in neighboring villages cannot understand each other.

Even today a definitive classification of the Mayance languages cannot be established because sufficient descriptive materials with regard to each of them. do not exist. Phonetic similarities between the languages must be determined, and then they must be analyzed from today backward in time, making comparative studies of the differences existing in each family. Such analyses are based on a linguistic technique called glottochronology that makes it possible to establish, with a reasonable degree of accuracy, the period in which each separated itself from the mother tongue (Proto-Maya), and the approximate date of later fractionations.

It is interesting to note that this technique is useful in history studies, since it permits us to identify the cultural differences acquired after separation, and such specific facts as mestizaje (whether voluntary or imposed by conquest) with other groups speaking tongues belonging to the same linguistic trunk.

Thus, the linguist first needs to establish the common

linguistic trunk by means of a phonologic matrix that makes it possible to group together the component languages. The latter are then subdivided into families. We shall see how this type of investigation enables us to attempt to explain why groups linguistically related now appear at points distant from the geographic area occupied by the majority of families of the same trunk, as has occurred with the Huastec.

By this method we can go even farther. When it is possible to trace, step by step, the dispersion and differentiation of Proto-Maya and subsequent further separation, and to follow the trail from languages still spoken back to their origin; when it is possible to distinguish between inherited linguistic material and that borrowed from other sources, then we shall have the history of the Maya culture as it appears reflected in its languages.

McQuown's classification is as follows:

A. Huastecan
   1. Huastec
      a. Veracruzano
      b. Potosino
   2. Chicomuceltec
B. Cholano
   1. Chontal
   2. Chol
   3. Chorti
C. Tzeltalan
   1. Tzeltal
   2. Tzotzil
   3. Toholabal
D. Chuh
E. Kanhobalan
   1. Jacaltec
   2. Kanhobal
   3. Solomec
F. Motozintlec
G. Mamean
   1. Mam
   2. Aguacatec
   3. Ixil
H. Quichean
   1. Rabinal
   2. Uspantec
   3. Quiché
   4. Cakchiquel
   5. Tzutuhil
I. Kekchian
   1. Kekchi
   2. Pokonchi
   3. Pokomam
J. Maya proper
   1. Yucatec
   2. Lacandón
   3. Itzá
   4. Mopan

McQuown himself says that a less cautious classification into subgroups would combine C, D and E; F and G; H and I.

Now, in what zones of present-day geographical divisions of the immense Maya territory are some of the languages listed still spoken?

The Chontal of Tabasco (another, but unrelated, Chontal is found in Oaxaca) is spoken in Chontalpa, a small area of four municipalities. In the greater part of Campeche, all of Yucatán and Quintana Roo, the northern half of Belize, and a portion of northern Guatemala, Yucatec is the language spoken.

Chol, Tzotzil, Tzeltal and Toholabal are spoken in Chiapas; along its border with Guatemala the tongues are Motozintlec and Lacandón, as well as a little Chuh and Jacaltec. Ixil, Tzutuhil, Kekchi, Quiché, Cakchiquel and other languages are spoken in Guatemala.*

THE HUASTEC ENIGMA

Another problem involved in Maya linguistic classification is that of the geographical and cultural separation of the Huastecs who, while their language forms part of macro-Maya, occupy a region very distant—parts of the states of Hidalgo, Veracruz, Tamaulipas, and San Luis Potosí. Many are the hypotheses advanced to clear up the problem, but as yet no thoroughly satisfactory solution has been found.

Let us set forth the elements of the enigma. If, as mentioned before, we can speak of a proto-Maya language, we can also refer to a proto-Maya community that, perhaps around 2600 B.C., existed in what is now the Department of Huehuetenango in northwest Guatemala.

---

* Maya is not as difficult to pronounce as it appears. The spelling of the written words is based, of course, on the Spanish interpretation of the sounds as they were first converted to our alphabet. Thus, vowel sounds are the same as in Spanish: *a*, ah; *e*, eh; *i*, ee; *o*, oh; *u*, oo. Consonants that have particular sounds are *c*, always pronounced as *k; h,* an aspirate; an apostrophe after *t*' and *p*' signals a glottal stop, an explosive sound; *k* is pronounced with a glottal stop whether or not it is followed by an apostrophe; *x* is pronounced *sh,* and *dz* is an explosive, lisping *ts*. Examples: Xlabpak, *Shlab-pahk*; Uxmal, *Oosh-mahl;* Ixchel, *Eesh-chehl;* Dzibilchaltún, *Tsee-beel-chahl-toon.*

At that time, and from that proto-Maya-community (thought to have been composed of some 5,000 persons), the dispersion of groups and the differentiation of the Maya language began. It is possible that a certain dialectal variation already existed among the members of that small group. We can assume all this thanks to present evidence from comparative Maya linguistic data.

Now, since the principal differentiation is to be found between Yucatec, Mam and Huastec, these three languages were probably the first to separate and differentiate from the proto-Maya of that community. Let's follow the trail of the Huastec.

Around 1800 B.C. the Huastec left the proto-Maya community and migrated to the northwest, perhaps to the Usumacinta drainage. The Yucatec went towards the same area, separating from the mother group a little later, around 1600 B.C., and maintained close contact with the Huastec until a break came about 1200 B.C., probably when the Huastec moved much farther northwest to the area they occupy today.

Comparative linguistics appear to demonstrate the foregoing. Other authors think that the separation came later, due to a wedge shoved between the Huastec and Maya areas by a Zoque group that still lives in northern Oaxaca-southern Chiapas. And the discussion goes on. . .

Marvelous bas-reliefs decorated door lintels in Yaxchilán. Here Yaxchilán ruler Bird Jaguar stands above a captive on this stone lintel dated February 19, 752 (not shown in drawing). The captive is identified by the cloth strips over his left arm, and what may be an earth-eating gesture of submission. The Late Classic period was one of increasing emphasis on warfare.

WHAT HAPPENED TO THE ANCIENT MAYA?

In the northern part of the state of Chiapas, over an extensive, high-lying area known as the Lacandón Jungle that extends eastward to El Petén, in Guatemala, there are many ruins of ancient Maya cities, cities that reached their peak during the period of Maya history called the Classic (200 - 1000 A.D.).

Archaeologists have calculated that at one time many tens of thousands of Maya lived within these centers. They have shown further that in the urban areas a great diversity of professional activities existed, as well as a marked social stratification, the priesthood and the nobility being directed by a king, the *Halach Uinic,* in whom was concentrated the exercise of earthly and spiritual powers.

At the end of the Classic period many cities, such as Bonampak, Yaxchilán and others, and the surrounding rural lands began to be abandoned (although centers such as Cobá and Chichén Itzá prospered and grew). While many reasons, both external and internal, have been suggested for the decline of those Maya cities, probably a complex interplay of factors was involved. Natural phenomena such as hurricanes or earthquakes would destroy food production but would not have affected so many areas. From skeletal remains, there is evidence of disease and malnutrition. Land exhaustion would have been a consequence of the inefficient slash and burn agriculture, increasingly augmented by intensive techniques perhaps a response to population increase. The production system may have simply become overburdened.

Such an internal decline could have been the stimulus for groups living on the periphery of the Maya area to move in. However, the changes in style reflecting Central Mexican models that appear in the Maya area in the Late Classic might well have resulted from alliance rather than conquest. The development of the sea trade routes, displacing the older overland ones, may have cut off lowland communities from critical economic resources and commerce. The philosophical system of the Maya has also been suggested as contributing to the demise of many of their cities. The emphasis on linking human history with cosmic events and cycles in the past may have induced such a sense of fatalism that effective steps were not taken to reverse growing problems.

But let us return to the cities in ruins found in Chiapas and Guatemala. Were they, in reality, completely abandoned, as consistently claimed in studies of the Maya? No, definitely not. Proof is to be found in the archives of Tabasco, Chiapas, Guatemala, and in Seville, Spain. When the Spaniards arrived numerous Maya groups had been occupying those cities for centuries, although the ancient Classic splendor had disappeared. In some places, the people lived around centers that had been constructed after the Classic period.

The drawing above reproduces in black and white one small scene from the extraordinary murals found at Bonampak. A replica of the temple and its murals may be viewed at the National Museum of Anthropology in Mexico City.

They spoke a number of languages, but all belonged to a common linguistic trunk, the Maya. In other words, in accordance with what anthropologists call the "genetic model," at some period in the past there had been a common historic tradition for, in addition to the related languages, they had two other factors in common: a way of life, and a physical type. It is true that on some stelae in the city of Seibal appear physical types distinct from the typical Maya, but that and other phenomena are testimony to foreign influence.

The interesting point is that the Lacandón Jungle and El Petén were heavily populated at the time the Spaniards appeared on the scene. Despite the relocation of human groups carried out by the conquerors, the wars, and the new European diseases that rapidly decimated the natives, today small groups descended from the pre-Hispanic peoples continue to inhabit the evergreen jungle. Innumerable cultural traits that archaeology tells us prevailed during the Classic period still persist, unchanged, among these present-day Maya, the Lacandón.

THE LACANDON

In reading this chapter, it is important to remember that an Indian group may be known by a popular name derived from the language or dialect spoken (Chol, Chorti, etc.), or from the name of the town or area it inhabits (Chamula, Zinacanteca, Lacandón). However, within the range of this book, all groups mentioned are Maya, unless specifically designated otherwise. The Lacandón to be discussed offer yet another name variant: they are known to outsiders as Lacandón, but refer to themselves as *Caribes* when speaking Spanish or *Hach Winik* when speaking Maya. Caribes was a name given to them by the Quiché and Cakchiquel Indians who accompanied the Spaniards, in the 16th century, during the first expeditions into the territory. For those Indians Carib was synonomous with cannibal or savage. Hach Winik, on the other hand, means "true man."

In giving special attention to the Lacandón we do so for the following reasons, and certainly *not* because the size of the group, compared to other present-day Maya peoples, warrants such treatment.

Their post-Conquest history is a tangled one and, in disentangling it, valuable information emerges that can be applied to deciphering life among the ancient Maya. The other side of the coin also becomes evident: the errors and misconceptions that can arise when such material is utilized indiscriminately to qualify, define and explain events and customs among the Maya more than a thousand years in the past.

And finally, we offer the Lacandón in evidence of what went on in the supposedly deserted jungles after the great Maya civilization collapsed.

The handful of human beings, known today as Lacandón, who inhabit the Chiapas jungle are not descendants of the large population so designated in the 16th and 17th centuries. Who are they? Where did they come from? What does a study of their present village culture contribute to shedding light on the magnificent Maya of the past?

Two errors greatly diminished the value of all work investigators had done on present-day Lacandón in an attempt to decipher their past. One was the use of a bibliography long regarded as classic for the study of any group by that name, meager, and now known to be of doubtful importance. For example, it has been shown that one of the books most frequently consulted, *The History of the Province of the Itzá* written by Juan de Villagutierre Sotomayor in 1700, once considered the number one historian of the region, was cribbed from many sources. Even worse, now that the majority of the works from which he took fragments have been identified, it is obvious that the author ignored other, extremely important information.

Firsthand investigation of colonial archives is the only way to overcome this deficiency—a long, hard, thankless task. Months of work result in a mere handful of facts, causing ethnohistorians to entrust it to other historians who, in turn and for the same reasons, prefer to leave it to the ethnohistorians. An endless circle leading nowhere, except to the hope that some day investigators prepared to eat the dust covering ancient documents will appear. By good fortune, someone has appeared in connection with the Lacandón—Nicholas Hellmuth who, after intensive research in archives of Guatemala and Mexico has provided significant clues.

The other error of scholars is that they attempted to reconstruct remote cultural elements, basing their efforts on accounts written in a much later period. That is, for instance, to describe the 9th century Maya civilization of Chiapas and El Petén lowlands in terms of Landa's Report on Yucatán's culture in the 16th century, so far removed both culturally and geographically.

To trace the post-Conquest history of those now referred to as Lacandón, therefore, we will utilize new facts revealed by Hellmuth's research.

Some authors are of the opinion that the term "Lacandón comes from *lacam-tun* (large rock) name that the Chol who inhabited the Lake Miramar area in the 16th century gave to the rocky island where their village was located. By deformation of the word, the Spanish conquerors called the Chol "Lacandón," thereby laying the basis for monumental future confusion because, from then on, the Spaniards referred to all groups found in the area as Lacandón. While undoubtedly all were Maya, they spoke different languages.

THE CHOL LACANDON

Captain Alonso Dávila, on a scouting expedition for Francisco de Montejo, conqueror of Yucatán, accidentally discovered the settlement of Lacam-tun in 1530. A member of the expedition described it: "...we arrived at a lagoon, 10 to 12 leagues in circumference and, in the center, an island with a town where there were some 60 houses of rich, warlike Indians."

Undoubtedly, these Indians spoke Chol and were the first to be referred to as Lacandón. In 1559, a Spanish army led by Pedro Ramírez Quiñones sacked and burned the town, taking some prisoners. In 1586, the Indians themselves destroyed it completely. A large Spanish force commanded by Juan de Morales Villavicencio had reached the shores of the lagoon, and the Indians, upon seeing them approach, preferred to destroy the town themselves, setting it afire and fleeing to the hills. Villavicencio then gave orders to destroy the crops under cultivation on the surrounding hillsides.

Memory of the terrible destruction of Lacam-tun was still alive in 1950 when archaeologist Frans Blom, on an expedition to Lake Miramar, relates that:

"From the confluence of the Jataté and Perlas rivers the Indians stubbornly refused to accompany expedition members up to the lake. They showed signs of fear and it appeared to concern the existence of a taboo among them. They told the mule drivers that once, long, long ago, many Caribes were killed by the 'pum-pum' (shotgun) in the Lake. They were acquainted with the Lake because they had viewed it several times from nearby hills, but roundly refused to approach its shores."

THE YUCATEC LACANDÓN

During the various incursions into the lowlands of Chiapas and Guatemala, principally those of 1530, 1559 and 1586 mentioned above, the Spaniards slaughtered probably half of the native population. Most of the remaining Indians, Chol-speaking, were forcibly resettled outside the area, and so by 1720 the region was nearly deserted. Thereafter began a migration of Yucatec-speaking Maya peoples, with groups coming from Tabasco, Campeche, Yucatán, and El Petén.

Those groups that began to fill the vacuum likewise received the name "Lacandón," although they spoke another language. And since the present-day Lacandón do not appear, either physically or culturally, to be descendants of the Chol-Lacandón, everything seems to indicate that they are descendants of the Yucatec peoples who arrived in the 17th and 18th centuries.

In the light of his investigations, Hellmuth says he is sure that the Yucatec Lacandón of a small 18th century mission settlement near Palenque, called San José de Gracia Real, are the direct ancestors of at least part of today's Lacandón, both north and south. He also says that the descriptions and surnames of the Lacandón of 1786-180(?)—duration of the San José mission—agree with those of the Lacandón since 1813 down to the present, taking into account, of course, the slow acculturation they have undergone due to increasingly frequent contacts with western culture.

Lacandóns Mateo and Chan Kin performing a healing ceremony in the temple of Naha. Behind them are the vessels representing the gods; the two in use symbolize Dzibaná and Akyanthó, gods of art, sculpture and foreigners. The gourd in front of Mateo holds copal for the ritual. Copal is a fragrant resin similar to frankincense. *Photo author.*

THE NAHA LACANDÓN

Only a few groups of Lacandón have survived, and they are scattered throughout the Chiapas jungle. Although until recently they numbered fewer than 200, today there are more than 300, leading me to believe, as stated by a contemporary author, that the Lacandón are struggling against nature in a process of adaptation that produces oscillations in their demography, and are not, as others state, on the verge of extinction. Those in Guatemalan territory disappeared in modern times.

The great cultural diversification existing among these 300 individuals is notable. Some northern groups, near important archaeological centers like Bonampak and Yaxchilán, have undergone such intensive contact with tourists, scientific investigators, itinerant traders and missionaries that they are frequently seen in western dress, preserving only a few polytheistic traits in their religion. They even speak a little English. Intensification of contact with western culture-bearers reached its height during the 1940's when thousands of *chicleros,* Mexican and foreign, entered their jungles to exploit the chicozapote trees from which chicle, the raw material of chewing gum, is obtained. This was before the substance was manufactured synthetically.

But one very conservative community, Naha, still exists. It is located in the area of three lovely lagoons—Xuux-Petá, Naha and K'an K'a Petá.

Food is abundant despite a marked decrease in the zone's wildlife. The Lacandón raise domestic fowl. Crops are varied and not, as many believe, limited to corn, although this grain is, as it has been for thousands of years, the principal staple. Small fish caught in the lagoons further diversify their diet.

ANCIENT GODS AND RITES PERSIST

Among the Naha Lacandón, religion continues to be polytheistic with a hierarchically structured pantheon headed by *Hach Chac Yum,* "True Lord (or Father) Chac (rain)." To pay homage to this deity the Lacandón make long pilgrimages to Yaxchilán, on the banks of the Usumacinta.

Like their pre-Hispanic ancestors, they divide the cosmos into various levels, on which they place their deities according to their functions. Among the gods ranking just below Hach Chac Yum are Akyanthó, Usukum and U'yidzin, his brothers. In a manner very similar to the human system, deities are organized by families, and by social classes, there being both lords and servants.

Akyanthó is the god of foreigners, of civilization and trade, according to Robert Bruce, who has done many of the best studies on Lacandón religion. *Usukum* lives in the bowels of the earth, in a cave. In addition to being the lord of the underworld, he is the bearer of the sun. He has as his servant *Kisin,* an abominable god, lord of evil spirits and producer of earthquakes who, it appears, inhabits the depths of Lake Naha. *U'yidzin* is the youngest brother, a good deity who dwells in Yaxchilán.

Other major deities are Kakoch, Ixkanleox, Akau, Mensabak, Itzana and Itzan Noh Ku.

Kakoch seems to be of great importance. Bruce believes him to be superior to Hach Chac Yum, and says that he is a remote god, creator of the earth, the sea, the first sun (not the "sun" or epoch in which we live) and of the *baknicté* or tuberose from which the primary gods were born. *Ixkanleox* was revered among the ancient Maya of Yucatán as the goddess of corn. The wife of Hach Chac Yum, according to Bruce, she created Lacandón women and things feminine, and set the world in order.

Akau, whose name means "the mother," is a maternal deity and thought to be the mother of various minor gods. Some consider her the moon and thus the wife of *Kin,* the sun. Under the name of Ixchel, she is the goddess of childbirth, a fact demonstrating the immutability of cultural traditions: from pre-Hispanic times, as reported by Landa, "at the time of their delivery, they resorted to sorceresses who made them believe their lies and placed beneath the bed an idol of the devil called *Ixchel* who, they said, was the goddess of conception."

Mensabak lives in the west and is the god of rain. According to Bruce, his name can be translated as "Maker of Gunpowder." *Sabak* originally meant "soot," but the Lacandón have applied it to gunpowder. With this substance, Mensabak's helpers make the black clouds that bear rain. The Lacandón priest who officiates in Mensabak's honor covers his tunic with soot from the smoke of copal burnt in the censers. He gathers

The Balché ceremony is perhaps the most important among present-day Lacandóns. Rites consist of consecrating and offering to the gods the traditional drink made from the bark of the balché tree, fermented with honey.

it by placing a gourd, representing the celestial vault, over the censer.

Itzana, says Bruce, is Kakoch's chief helper, and also lives in Yaxchilán. *Itzan Noh Ku* (Great God Lizard), and Itzana, constitute an important pair of gods because their names may derive from Itzamná, principal deity among the pre-Hispanic Yucatec Maya. Unfortunately, little has been learned about the two. But we do know that, according to the Lacandón, Itzan Noh Ku dwells in Lake Pet-ha to the north, where there is a painting that represents a two-headed serpent. Interesting because, as Eric Thompson says, the Itzamnás who can be represented as a saurian or a serpent "generally have a second head at the rear of the body."

As in other zones of the ancient Maya area, the Lacandón portray their gods in the form of semispherical clay bowls with the face of the deity on the front. The bowls are fragile due to lack of firing, the Lacandón having forgotten how their ancestors used kilns. Too, the paints they employ are inferior, mere vegetable pigments, erasable by light rubbing. But with these paints, the name of the deity can be "written" with symbols, according to the key discovered by Bruce.

Rare now is the use of the sacred tunic. It was made by beating the bark of the *mahaua* tree into a sort of cloth from which the garment was sewn up. Then it was painted with symbols in various colors. Ritual objects still in use include the sacred canoe in which the traditional and millennial ceremonial drink, *balché,* is prepared; gourd cups, often ornamented with symbols, for drinking the liquor; the wooden slabs with copal pellets pressed onto them; the low benches or *canchés;* the gourds in which the copal is melted, and dolls made of rubber as in pre-Hispanic times, used for offerings. With these and other appurtenances the Lacandón carry out their religious ceremonies in the temple, an immense hut without walls. There they call to the gods, first with a conch shell or drum, then with ancient prayers. As examples, the following were collected by Alfred M. Tozzer more than 70 years ago, and remain practically unchanged today.

Prayer during an eclipse of the sun

"Oh Lord, the most excellent, do not allow this fire to disappear. Come forth, to the heat, later I shall fulfill my obligations to thee, Oh Lord, the most excellent. Look, come out, come to the warmth. I, although poor, look upon the most excellent. It is oppressed. I am not mistaken. I am continent, Oh Lord, I have no relations with anyone, not even my own family, Oh Lord . . ."

Purification of the pom (copal) grains

"May it break! May it shatter! I burn thee. Live! Awaken! Sleep not! Work! I am he who awakens thee to life. I am he who lifts thee up to life, within the receptacle. I am he who revives thee. I am he who awakens thee to life. I am he who lifts thee up to life. I am he who fashions thy bones. I am he who fashions thy head. I am he who fashions thy lungs. I am he who fashions thee, thy maker."

This mask set into the center of the access stairway to a temple at Comalcalco is an example of the sensitive, refined modeling in stucco characteristic of many Maya sites. Identification of the motif is difficult because the defining information, contained in the headdress, has been eroded. The stucco style at Late Classic Comalcalco is similar to that found at the larger site of Palenque only 100 miles away.

TRAVELING INTO THE MAYA AREA

Well into the state of Tabasco, eastward on Highway 180, in the region of the Chontalpa or place of the *chontalli* (the Putún-Maya), is the town of Cárdenas, at a crossroads.

North from Cárdenas over Highway 187 it is only 25 miles to the ruins of Comalcalco, in pre-Hispanic times the westernmost city in Maya territory. Surrounded by groves of cacao trees, this is a site not mentioned in the usual tourist guides, but now well worth a visit because archaeological explorations have recently been intensified.

COMALCALCO

Although discovered in 1880 by Désiré Charnay, little was known about Comalcalco until it was visited by Frans Blom and Oliver La Farge in 1925. Their observations and discoveries were published the following year in the book *Tribes and Temples.*

Like all sites in the Chontalpa, Comalcalco presents a strange combination of Maya Classic and non-Classic elements. Absent, for instance, is the typical Classic portrayal of human features: deformed, flattened forehead, prominent nose, drooping lower lip, and receding chin.

This combination of elements is clearly apparent in the tomb discovered by Blom and La Farge in 1925. The sanctuary, adorned with nine personages in stucco relief, adjoins the mound they called the Palace, near Temple 2. It came to light when they were about to leave the ruins, believing their work to be finished. The theme is suggestive of the nine lords of the underworld, but Blom's interpretation is totally different. It was his opinion that the central personage on the east wall (the figures are distributed in groups of three, accompanied by columns of hieroglyphs, on the north, south and east walls) represents the man buried in the chamber and that all the others, whose poses and dress he described, form part of the dignitary's entourage. He even identified one of the figures as a buffoon, and Landa says that the governors had buffoons at court.

Unique in Comalcalco are two building materials: oyster shells in immense quantities used for fill and ornamentation, and bricks or blocks of sun-baked clay employed much as we do today. This is interesting because it had been thought that bricks were a Spanish import, the product of Arab influence in Spain.

Two principal groups of structures compose the central area, one around a great pyramid topped by a temple, and the other, various edifices placed on an artificial platform. In 1960 another structure was discovered, ornamented with great stucco masks on the panels and stairway. Especially notable are masks of the sun god.

VILLAHERMOSA

Returning to Cárdenas and continuing east on Highway 180, it is 32 miles to Villahermosa, capital of Tabasco. We know practically nothing about the Maya past of Villahermosa and its environs. But a visit to two places in the city: La Venta Park and CICOM (Research Center for Olmec and Maya Cultures), will give a very good idea of the Maya's predecessor in the region — the so-called "Mother Culture," the Olmec, (1200-400 B.C.) and some masterworks are on display.

Within the CICOM complex, located on the shore of the Grijalva River, is the Regional Anthropology Museum, named for native son, the poet Carlos Pellicer. The museum has several Maya rooms with some truly unique exhibits: a series of small objects, among them the famous figurines of Jonuta and Jaina, a magnificent ceramics collection, including the Pellicer Vase, painted with a scene of princes on a terrace; a series of stucco masks from Palenque; stupendous stelae from Balankan in the Usumacinta basin; and copies of the mural paintings at Bonampak.

With this museum and that of La Venta Park, to which he transported all the large sculptures threatened by oil drilling activities at the nearby site of La Venta, Carlos Pellicer, their promotor, museographer and Maecenas, authored two of his loveliest compositions.

PALENQUE

From Villahermosa, the drive to Palenque in the state of Chiapas requires a little more than two hours —and best the traveler prepare himself for an incomparable experience. After a short distance over a winding road through the jungle, Temples XII and XIII, the Temple of the Inscriptions, and the southern part of the Palace appear before his eyes.

A little later, from the Central Plaza and in front of the Temple of the Inscriptions, a wondrous view of almost the entire city is spread before him: the Temples of the Sun, the Cross of Palenque, and the Foliated Cross; the remains of Temple X, the Temple of the Count, and the five temples of the North.

The most eye-arresting structure is the monumental Temple of the Inscriptions, and it has a fascinating story. It was constructed in the purest Palencano style, one of the several Maya architectural styles. Four of them will be described in the chapter on Yucatán; here we will take up two others, Palencano and El Petén.

El Petén style is characterized by stepped terraces, sloping corners, stairways that stand out over the surface of the structure, and great stucco masks used for decoration. Solid masses predominate over open spaces in the shrine-temples atop the pyramids. Massive, lofty roof crests were constructed over the rear wall of temples. Cities typifying this style are Tikal, Uaxactún, and Piedras Negras.

However, in the Palencano style (named for its principal exponent, Palenque), the temples surmounting

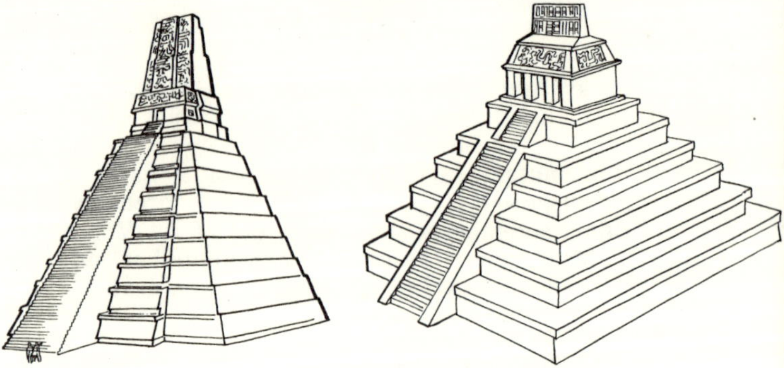

Left, the best examples of the Petén style of Maya architecture are to be found in Tikal. The monumental proportions can be appreciated in comparison with the figures at the bottom of the stairway. The pyramid temple, right, is representative of the Palencano style.

the pyramid bases are composed of two galleries, the rear one being the sanctuary. Here, airiness and open spaces prevail over heavy masses. The open-work roof crests rest on the middle of the temple roof. In addition to Palenque, the centers most representative of this style are Yaxchilán and Bonampak.

It appears that Palenque was inhabited from the first century A.D., reaching its peak about the sixth century. In the 9th or 10th century it was abandoned, probably following invasion of peoples from the Gulf of Mexico.

Palenque lay hidden in the jungle until the 18th century when, after it had been visited by several travelers, Capt. José Antonio del Río in 1786 was ordered by Spanish King Charles III to report on it. In 1805 Guillermo Dupaix, in the service of the Spanish Crown, was enjoined to explore the city. His study, illustrated by Mexican artist Luciano Castañeda, appeared in 1834. A few years later Austrian Baron Frederic Waldeck, lived in the ruins for two years. And in 1841 appeared the magnificent book by American author John L. Stephens, *Incidents of Travel in Central*

America, Chiapas and Yucatán, including a visit to Palenque, and illustrated with the extraordinary, almost photographic, drawings of Englishman Frederick Catherwood.

It was not until 1925, however, that a good map of the zone was produced by Frans Blom, and not until 1940 that exploration was undertaken. Alberto Ruz L. discovered the incredible tomb in the Temple of the Inscriptions in 1952.

THE ROYAL TOMB

In the rear gallery of this temple, in 1949, Ruz came upon an immense paving stone with orifices stopped up by stone plugs. Raising the stone, he found a staircase leading down into the interior of the pyramid. The stairwell was completely blocked with rocks that the Maya undoubtedly had placed there to prevent violation of the sepulchral chamber. So successful had they been that Ruz needed four seasons of work (only in the dry season is work possible) to gain access. Finally, at the foot of the stairway, his way was blocked by a massive triangular stone. It was removed and Alberto Ruz has vividly described his impressions upon finally entering the marvelous burial chamber:

"... I found myself in a spacious crypt that appeared to have been carved in ice—the walls were covered with a brilliant calcareous layer, stalactites hung from the ceiling like curtains, thick stalagmites resembling huge tapers rose from the floor, all limestone formations caused by the filtration of rain water through the body of the pyramid for more than a thousand years. The crypt measures nearly 30' by 13'. The apex of the vaulted ceiling is 23' from the floor, reinforced by immense beams of polished stone, black with yellow veining, that look like wood. The chamber was so perfectly constructed that the centuries have not affected it even though it supports the entire weight of the pyramid and temple.

"... Around the walls, human figures modeled in stucco appear to stand guard: nine priests depicted slightly larger than life. Six are standing, three seated . . . Some of these stupendous stucco reliefs are well preserved, but others have been partially destroyed by the extreme humidity of the crypt. It is likely that they represent the nine lords of the shadowy darkness, guardians of the nine lower worlds of Maya mythology.

". . . Most amazing is the colossal monument that occupies most of the space. A great sculptured tablet, measuring 12'6" by 7'4", rested on a monolithic block. The weight of the whole, approximately 22 tons, was borne by six monolithic supports, four of which were sculptured.

". . . Our first impression was that it might be a ceremonial altar, preserved in this secret place far from the public eye for some religious reason. We decided then that if further exploration did not furnish new information, the crypt must have been the most sacred sanctuary of the Palencanos. This meant that if it were an altar, the monolith under the tablet had to be solid and its function merely that of a base. But there was another possibility: that it might be hollow and therefore not an altar. The tablet weighs some five tons and, because of its magnificent bas-reliefs, constitutes one of the masterpieces of Maya art. To raise it presented certain difficulties and dangers. The chief problem was one of space in which to use machinery and the impossibility of introducing such machinery into the crypt. Without lifting the tablet, therefore, I wished to ascertain whether the block was hollow. In areas not sculptured I ordered the block to be bored, on a horizontal plane toward the center. The first probing was without result since the workman inclined his drill downward, reaching the center without finding anything but stone. In another probing the drill penetrated a cavity, and a wire introduced through the hole, upon being withdrawn, showed traces of red paint.

"The moment in which I verified that the supposed base of the hypothetical altar was hollow, like the moment of discovery of the crypt, was one of tremendous excitement. It might have been a huge receptacle for offerings, but the size and form of the monument, as well as the presence of red paint, promised something else. In the Maya cosmogony,

The Temple of the Inscriptions was so named because of the long inscription of 620 hieroglyphs on panels within the temple. The cut-away view shows placement of the inner stairway and tomb. Pacal, Palenque's greatest ruler, who reigned in the seventh century A.D. and brought the city to its zenith, is buried in the tomb.

red is associated with the East and almost always appears in tombs—on the walls, on funerary offerings, on the human remains. The East is the region where every day the sun is born anew after its daily death in the West. The East, therefore, is the place of resurrection, and the red that symbolizes it, placed in tombs, presages immortality. The tablet, then, had to be raised despite difficulties and dangers. Using truck jacks placed on tree trunks and below the corners of the tablet, we lifted it. Introducing the trunks into the crypt, their proper placement, and the delicate operation of raising the tablet took 24 consecutive hours which I spent in the crypt without leaving it, from 6:00 a.m. November 27, 1952, to the same hour on the 28th.

"As the tablet began to rise, I could see there was a cavity carved in the monolith . . . A polished stone slab sealed it perfectly; the slab had four perforations, each sealed by a large stone plug. As soon as space permitted, I slid between the tablet and the slab, lifted out one of the plugs, and flashed my electric torch into the opening. A few inches from my eyes appeared a human skull covered with pieces of jade.

"By passing ropes through the holes we removed the slab in a maneuver that must have been similar to the one used by the priests in placing it. The mortuary cavity appeared with its impressive contents, in a setting of vivid vermilion for the walls and floor of the cavity are covered with cinnabar. The skeleton rested in a normal position, arms and legs extended, face up. The bones crumbled to the touch due to the humidity, but were in place. We were able to determine that the skeleton was of a man 40 to 50 years of age, tall, robust and well proportioned, without apparent pathological lesions. The state of destruction of the skull prevented our being able to tell if it had been artificially deformed as was the custom among Maya nobles and priests.

"... Against the red background of the coffin and the bones covered with cinnabar, the brilliant green of jade stood out, for the personage had been buried with all his jade jewels... diadem... earplugs... necklace... breastplate... bracelets... and jade figurines... At the moment of burial his face had been covered by a jade mosaic mask, the pieces being stuck to a thin layer of stucco applied to the face. We found some fragments adhering to the stucco and the rest had slipped to the left of the head. With the aid of photographs and drawings made during the exploration, it was possible to reconstruct the mask which probably portrays to some degree the living features of the corpse.

"... It is to be assumed that the dignitary interred was the same person who planned and ordered construction of the gigantic mausoleum. After he was buried, the sarcophagus sealed and the sculptured tablet lowered into position, the priests placed on the tablet other symbols of his office: a belt adorned with three tiny jade masks and nine slate pendants in the form of hatchets; a shield with a figure of the sun god; and what was probably a scepter, with a mask of the rain god.

"... The crypt was then closed, and six young men, in all likelihood sons of nobles, were sacrificed to accompany the prince to the other world. Finally, they filled up the stairway to the floor of the temple, depositing various offerings along the way. But if, materially, access to the tomb was sealed off forever, spiritually there remained a bond: from the sarcophagus to the temple threshold, a stucco serpent undulated along the steps, a kind of molding that was at the same time a hollow conduit, magic means of maintaining communication with the illustrious deceased, probably deified prince and priest.

"Discovery of the Royal Tomb in the Temple of the Inscriptions caused a sensation for various reasons: its unusual location under the pyramid; communication with the temple; its dimensions, solidity and excellent construction; extraordinary stucco reliefs: colossal sepulchre covered by symbolic and chronological reliefs of magnificent workmanship and enormous importance; burial of a high-ranking personage with all of his jewels. This discovery demonstrated that the American pyramid was not necessarily and exclusively a solid base to support a temple, as previously believed, in opposition to the Egyptian pyramid ..."*

TEMPLE XIII TOMB

During excavations in mid-1994 adjacent to the Temple of the Inscriptions, another splendid tomb nearly as important as that found in 1952, was discovered in the substructure of Temple XIII. Again, it was not a simple burial but that of a person of high rank interred in a sarcophagus within a mortuary chamber. The skeleton was that of a tall, robust female who lived about 1200 years ago. She was adorned with jewelry, mask and headdress, all of jade. With the discovery of this second magnificent tomb it seems almost certain that the Great Plaza, bordered on one

---

* From *La civilización de los antiguos Mayas,* by Alberto Ruz Lhuillier. INAH, México, D.F., 1963.

side by the Temple of the Inscriptions and Temple XIII, served as a necropolis for the ruling class.

The tomb of Pacal, Palenque's great seventh century sovereign in the Temple of the Inscriptions, is open to visitors. The identity of the occupant of the Temple XIII tomb is under study, and access to the tomb may be restricted.

Below, the accession of Kan Xul, second of Pacal's sons to succeed him, is portrayed on a stone tablet, dated to about A.D. 721, in the Palace at Palenque. Kan Xul, center, is flanked by his father on the left, and his mother Lady Ahpo Hel, on the right. He is dressed simply because he is not yet king. Both his father and his mother are dead at the time of the actual accession but are depicted in the act of presenting their son with important symbolic items of Maya rulership. Pacal gives the headdress to his son who leans toward his father to receive it, while his mother holds a bowl with an eccentric flint and a shield. After he was dressed as king, Kan Xul would have presented himself to the people.

Pacal, after reigning in Palenque for many years, died in A.D. 683 and Chan-Bahlum was the first of his sons to succeed him. Right, Chan-Bahlum as depiced in one panel of a stone tablet, dated to 692, in the rear room of the Temple of the Cross. He is dressed in the traditional Maya costume of kings. Many scholars believe that Chan-Bahlum is buried in the Temple of the Cross, following in the tradition of his father Pacal whose spectacular tomb was found in the Temple of the Inscriptions.

CAMPECHE, AND THE CONSERVATIVE MAYA

Although the city of Campeche, principal port and now capital of Campeche state, was the first important Spanish settlement on the Peninsula, it was never the seat of a *Capitanía General.* This was probably due to fear that the city might be occupied by pirates (as it was several times), the authorities imprisoned and, therefore, unable to pay tribute to the Crown. The Capitanía was always located inland, in the city of Mérida, and between Campeche and Mérida a road was constructed, then as now called *El Camino Real,* the Main or Principal Road.

At the time of the Conquest, the present state of Campeche was divided into chieftainships, the most important being that of the Ah Canul, a family of Mexican origin who had been granted the area by the Maya rulers of Uxmal, Chichén Itzá and Mayapán. The greater part of the Camino Real traverses the former domains of the Ah Canul.

Following the old route, the modern highway begins about 19 miles east of Campeche, at Chencoyi. The first village thereafter is Tinum, on whose outskirts are still to be seen some Maya potter families who have taken up beekeeping in recent years, apparently with success. Then come Tenabo, Pomuch and Hecelchakan, all with the occasional Maya hut interspersed among masonry houses. In Hecelchakan there is a handsome museum with an excellent collection of the famous ceramics of Jaina, an island off the Campeche coast where the pre-Hispanic Maya had a large cemetery. There the dead

Figurine from Jaina. The Island of Jaina, off the coast of Campeche, was an ancient Maya cemetery where, in the hundreds of graves, many figurines like this one were found. Richly colored, they depicted personages and scenes that have enriched our knowledge of the Maya. Examples can be seen in the museum at Hecelchakan together with a strong collection of stone sculpture, including ruler portraits and glyphic inscriptions, which is in the garden. The museum closes for siesta in the afternoon.

were accompanied by numerous offerings, among which the "portrait" figures are outstanding.

Next is Calkiní, one of the principal settlements in the Ah Canul domain, with a notable fortress monastery founded by the Franciscans in 1555. Following is Becal where the famous jipi-japa hats are made, similar to and as fine as the well-known Panama. Worth visiting are the caves the Indians have excavated in the limestone rock under their houses. There, underground, they weave the hats so that the fiber, a reed plant called *jipi,* will preserve the necessary humidity.

Finally, Halachó in the state of Yucatán, a village where basketry ornamented with motifs of Central Mexican origin is produced; an example of the persistence of cultural traditions for these elements entered the Maya area more than one thousand years ago.

The trip just completed and the one that follows are of special interest: along these two routes is to be found a concentration of the conservative Maya who guard traditions reaching back to pre-Hispanic times.

Our second trip starts from Ticul, Yucatán, the Peninsula's leading ceramics center with potters at work everywhere. There are goldsmiths, too, and while the visitor waits and watches they can fashion a set of buttons to adorn one of the beautiful Yucatecan shirts or *guayaberas*. In this village still live descendants of the Xiú, the noble family that governed Uxmal during the closing years of its pre-Conquest splendor.

Continuing southeast, we find Oxkutzcab set in the middle of extensive orange groves, and in Peto there is a Coordinating Center of the National Indian Institute which, using the techniques of applied anthropology, labors to bring about the integration of Indians into the national culture without destroying their own worthwhile cultural elements. Visitors are welcome.

Just before reaching Carrillo Puerto, in Quintana Roo, visit the two Maya villages of Xiatil and Dzulá near the highway. Dzulá is an example of what can be achieved through acculturation. In a single generation, the village has passed from a conservative culture to one where many of the inhabitants possess masonry houses, refrigerators; the girls have permanents and gold teeth (the latter more frequently as a symbol of prestige than from necessity); and all have lost the aggressiveness that characterized the Indians of this area at the turn of the century.

The route ends at Carrillo Puerto, formerly the sacred city of Chan Santa Cruz, capital of the Indian rebels who fought the War of Castes in the 19th century. Still standing, almost intact, is the church which housed the talking cross that directed the war. (See p. 67).

THE CONSERVATIVE MAYA

Not all areas of the immense Yucatán Peninsula have been studied ethnographically. But sufficient knowledge has been accumulated to establish a series of culture patterns that aid in identifiying and defining the most conservative Maya groups—conservatism ranging from monolingualism to the physical appearance of the villages.

Robert Redfield, in a very fair analysis, summed it up by declaring that to define an element of contemporary culture on the Peninsula as "Indian" is to say it represents a continuity of tradition that existed in Yucatán before the arrival of the Spaniards. He also noted that the present culture of Yucatán is an integrated and unified way of life representing neither the pre-Hispanic Indian culture, nor the Spanish, nor the sum of both, but a new development—result of the first contact with the Conquest.

KINSHIP

Let us then consider the characteristics of some Indian culture patterns, beginning with the systems of kinship and religion. These same patterns also apply to Belize, for the population of that English colony, at least in its northern section, is made up principally of descendants of Maya who, toward the end of the past century, fled from Mexican government troops, crossed the Río Hondo and took refuge around Corozal.

Great differences exist between the present kinship system and that of the pre-Hispanic Maya. The latter appears to have been based on a structure of clans and lineages, a situation which endured, at least to some extent, on the Peninsula until the 18th century due to a certain cohesion within lineages. (The system still exists in Chiapas among Tzotzil- and Tzeltal-speaking groups.) Persons bearing the same surname formed part of a large family and were therefore considered to be members of the same lineage; and persons with the same surname were forbidden to intermarry. The surname was transmitted paternally and, as the important bond, it was only through the male lineage that one was entitled to belong to a "company" or to inherit the family cross.

Although this tradition was strictly observed into the 18th century, the Indians, on into the 19th, continued taking into account the quality of nobility that distinguished these lineages, conferring upon their members the title of *Ah mehenob* (Knights or Nobles) as well as the right to hold the highest posts in local government.

COMPANY AND CROSS

A "company" is one band of those that make up a subtribe (like that of the X-Cacal in Quintana Roo, described by Alfonso Villa Rojas). The cross is the holiest and most important symbol, perpetuator of the "speaking idols" that served as oracles for the ancient Maya. Crosses in the principal native temples, located in the head villages, continued to speak until a generation ago, and the faithful were permitted to listen to them in order to receive the divine message.

Modern descriptions show that the family pattern now predominant is that of the parental family, composed of father, mother, children, and sometimes a very close relative of the spouses. This is in contrast to the group conscience among members of the same lineage or of the multiple families of the past that now are found only occasionally in remote villages. Group conscience was acquired as a result of patriarchal authority and the custom of grouping the huts of married offspring around that of the father.

Although today kinship is most commonly expressed in bilateral terms (a custom of European origin whereby the individual bears both paternal and maternal surnames), in Quintana Roo there are vestiges of the ancient form. And further vestiges could be found upon investigation. Why? Because some subtribes have reformed. Groups that had chosen "the way of progress" later rejected it, returning to the sparsely inhabited mountain areas in an attempt to re-create their ancient way of life.

GODPARENTS AND BAPTISM

Godparent relationships, *compadrazgos,* are extremely important throughout the Peninsula, but especially among the most conservative groups. Immediately after a baby is born (in Quintana Roo a woman gives birth in a squatting position as in pre-Conquest times), and after the umbilical cord has been cut with a blade made from a section of a reed plant called *halal* so that the mother is not "chilled" by the "cold" of the scissors, the child's baptism is planned.

This ceremony is performed generally throughout the Peninsula—in isolated communities by the High Priest or *Nohoch-Tata* who resides in the head village. The godparent relationship is established at that time, but no one expresses a preference as to the child's name inasmuch as the baby is always named for the Catholic patron saint of that day: one name if birth takes place before noon, another if after midday, for noon rather than midnight signals the date change in traditional communities.

In other areas the godparent relationship is a weaker tie; scissors are used to cut the umbilical cord, and baptism is performed by a Catholic priest.

Another ceremony of great importance in ancient times—now on the wane—also created a godparent relationship: the *hetz mek,* a symbolic awakening of the child's skills. At the appropriate age the godfather —or godmother, depending on the child's sex—places the child astraddle his hip, the way children are always carried in the Maya area. Several turns are made around a table displaying objects indicative of the adult activities of the child's sex, and he or she is instructed as to their use.

DEITIES, OLD AND NEW

The presence of a *H'men* or Prayermaker is required in almost all these ceremonies. A sort of priest-shaman, he performs the most important rites, like the propitiatory rites of the fields asking for good rains and abundant crops. Many of them are carried out within village. churches, but others, like the *cha-chaac* (summoning of the *chaacs* or rain gods), the *oxdias* (*ox,* three in Maya; *días,* days in Spanish), and that of *okotbatam* (plea) are performed in the fields.

Many ceremonies are accompanied by Catholic prayers and rites. In communities not visited by priests, the rites are performed by Indians called "Master

Singers." Villages are conceived of as squares, marked off from the surrounding bush — domain of the supernaturals — by crosses at the four corners. Today, the crosses have saints' names and serve to protect the inhabitants of the village against evil, human, animal or supernatural. This is an ancient practice, pre-dating Christianity, when sacred trees served to ward off evil.

Religious syncretism is in evidence everywhere; for example, in this prayer pronounced during the okotbatam that renders homage to many of the gods and spirits of the presentday Maya pantheon. The okotbatam is the most significant and elaborate ceremony of the agricultural cycle, performed yearly at the time of the corn's peak growth, in August or September.

God the Father, God the Son, God the Holy Ghost,
Kanleox, lovely lady, and thou
lovely lady *Madalena,* and thou
lovely lady *Verónica,* and thou
lovely lady *Guadalupe.*
Here I call upon ye to gather, where majesty resides,
the Holy Lords
Lord Zaztunchac in the east,
Yaxpapatun, Chacpapatun, Kanpapatun,
Ekpapatun, Kakalmozonikob,
Mizencaanchauc, Ah Thoxoncaanchaac,
San Miguel Arcángel, Boloncaanchaac,
Lelemcaanchaac, Hohopcaanchaac.
May ye all be glorified
while my words are pronounced for
the protectors of the land, the protector
of the woods, the protector of the plains,
the protector of the mountain.
So I direct my words to where
ye reside, ye are placed by
God the Father, God the Holy Ghost.

This prayer, pronounced in Maya, is worth analyzing for it helps to understand a syncretistic process as well as Maya religious thought. The words italicized signal the most obvious interpolations. In addition, however, the Spanish word *Dios* (God) is used in the original accompanied by the Maya words *yumbil* (Lord or Father), *mehenbil* (son), and the Spanish *Espíritu Santo* (Holy Ghost). Other Spanish words used in the text are Madalena, Verónica, Guadalupe, and San Miguel Arcángel (St. Michael Archangel).

After the Conquest Catholic saints were substituted for some Maya gods, but the substitution *was not total.* The Maya continued "thinking" about their old gods but called them by other names. Thus, for example, the Christian Trinity was identified, like the pre-Hispanic *Pahuatuns* ("papatun" in the prayer text), with the winds and the cardinal directions.

The text quoted begins by naming the Trinity, two Catholic saints and the Virgin Mary in her Mexican guise, Santa María de Guadalupe. In this case, none of them appears to be a substitution for the Pahuatuns inasmuch as those deities are cited immediately thereafter and given a color, in accordance with pre-Hispanic cosmovision which placed each Pahuatun as the Lord of a cardinal point of the universe with its corresponding color.

For instance, yellow denotes the south and the place of a female deity—X'Kanleox ("She of the Yellow-Leafed Food:" Goddess of Corn), mentioned in the text. The Maya often replace her with Mary Magdalene. The red Pahuatun is located in the east, and is St. Dominic; to the north is the white, St. Gabriel; the black to the west is St. James.

Names of the other Maya gods cited in the text translate as follows: *Zaztunchac,* Rain God Transparent Stone; *Yaxpapatun,* First Pahuatun or First Rockbreaker; *Chacpapatun,* Red Pahuatun (Rockbreaker); *Kanpapatun,* Yellow Pahuatun; *Ekpapatun,* Black Pahuatun; *Kakalmozonikob,* Gods of the Fire and of the Whirlwind; *Mizencaanchauc,* Lightning Bolt that Sweeps the Heavens; *Ah Thoxoncaanchaac,* Our Rain God of the Third Heaven; *Boloncaanchaac,* Rain God of the

Ninth Heaven; *Lelemcaanchaac,* Rain God of the Flashing Whip; *Hohopcaanchaac,* Rain God of the Fifth Heaven. A curious note is the placement of St. Michael among the chaacs or rain gods.

The Prayermaker continues by naming other gods, of supreme importance to agriculture—protectors of the land, the woods, the plains and the mountain. And these are not by any means the only gods still worshiped. For the Maya, the woods, the air, the darkness are full of mysterious beings ever ready to harm or to serve them. Of greatest consequence are the *Yumtzilob* (Lords or Patrons), deities charged with overseeing and protecting human actions with respect to nature, the fields, and the rains.

In the cha-chaac rites at Spring's end, therefore, the most elaborate and spectacular ceremony still performed by the Maya, the good offices of the Yumtzilob are sought. The ritual altar represents the earth that, according to ancient belief, was flat and square. The boughs and vines that adorn it are all "cold" (in the medieval sense) as is the rain for which the supplicants are praying. Human participants in the ceremony represent some of the deities invoked, as well as the birds and aquatic animals, like the frogs, that announce the advent of rain. Other deities protect the animals important to the Maya, like the bee, deer, etc.

Today, fiestas dedicated to the Catholic patron saint of the village have replaced a number of these ceremonies. And some conservative Indians who observe their okotbatam, cha-chaac and oxdias also attend the *vaquerías* or gay celebrations in honor of the patron saints.

HOME AND HEARTH

The appearance of the villages is indicative of another cultural pattern that demonstrates the differences between traditional and modern. In pre-Hispanic times, while many Maya cities supported populations of 50,000 within the urban area through intensive agricul-

The typical Yucatecan hut has not changed in thousands of years. The same design was used for the stone temples.

ture in the form of raised fields along rivers and in swampy areas, large numbers of people lived at a considerable distance from the cities following a scattered-settlement pattern in which each dwelling was built near the land the family farmed.

Upon the arrival of the Spaniards, to facilitate conversion to Christianity and effect absolute subjection, an attempt was made to gather the Indians in European-style towns, with living quarters grouped in blocks around a plaza where buildings housed the civil and religious authorities. But results were not always satisfactory; many Indian villages are still formed in a scattered pattern. The occasional group of huts is due to the kinship system. The same occurs with respect to the appearance of the houses. Traditionally, the floor plan is almost oval, and dwellings are built of palm (the roof) and *bajareque* (logs or reeds joined together, smoothed over with mud and then calcimined), while those of wealthier individuals are of masonry and cement in the usual provincial style.

Furnishings also provide an indication of the degree of traditionalism. Metal cooking ware and dishes acquired in the cities are little by little replacing clay ware—jars, plates, water jugs—often made within the household, as well as gourd utensils. The bags or henequen nets, the hammock, the small, low benches called *canché,* and the three-stone hearth fire ring are also disappearing.

Fire is still venerated in Quintana Roo, where a ceremony similar to the Aztec New Fire is performed. The hearth fire must be kept burning throughout the year until Good Friday, when it is allowed to go out. The "new fire" is kindled on the following day, Holy Saturday.

GOING MODERN

And finally, the style of dress is an indicator. Sandals (a very famous type is the *chirriador* or "squeaker" used to dance the gala *jarana*) are being replaced by western-style shoes. The same is happening with the lovely embroidered *huipil* (a long, loose, square-necked overblouse) of the Yucatecan mestiza, and with the white pantaloons and high-collared shirts of the men. All are giving way to western-style clothing.

A truly contradictory note is struck by the sight of Maya-speaking Indians listening to a transistor radio, or a TV antenna sprouting from the palm roof of a hut that is far beyond the reach of any video channel.

A Yucatecan mestiza in her traditional *huipil*. The white underskirt, decorated with embroidery or lace, hangs several inches below the edge of the huipil.

MERIDA, MONUMENTS, AND MARVELOUS FOOD IN YUCATAN

Mérida, capital of the state of Yucatán, is a lovely city. It was founded on the ruins of the Maya city of T'Hó in 1542. The Cathedral, on the main plaza, although subsequently modified, dates from the 16th century. From the same period is the Montejo House, built by the Conquistador; the beauty of its plateresque facade has been preserved intact. Plateresque, too, is Las Monjas or the Convent of the Nuns, with a tower that terminates in a balcony, a cool, open walkway.

Good hotels and places of entertainment are numerous, for Mérida is a gay city and has produced musicians of international fame like Ricardo Palmerín and Armando Manzanero. Traditional dances, especially the *jarana,* are performed often — at public ceremonies, in night clubs and restaurants — and the beat of modern rhythms is also present.

The Maya culture is evident, too, in places like the Ermita, a church in whose garden pre-Columbian sculptures are displayed, or the Regional Museum of Archaeology, with its magnificent collection. Touring the city in a *calesa* or horse-drawn carriage is a delightful experience.

But let's leave the city behind and be off to adventure on the trail of ancient history. To the south, 10 miles from Mérida, is the town of Uman. We'll take time to refresh ourselves with a Yucatecan soft drink, *horchata,* made of ground rice and almonds, because throughout the Peninsula the heat is oppressive, except in the winter months. But no matter, there is so much to see.

Twenty-seven miles beyond is Muna with its unforgettable, monumental fortress-type church constructed shortly after the Conquest, and we are only 10 miles

from the ruins of Uxmal; those of Kabah lie a short distance beyond. Now we can savor the extraordinary reality of the Maya culture.

Uxmal and Kabah share in the architectural styles known as Puuc and Chenes. And these two styles reveal influences from the Río Bec.

The Río Bec style is characterized by buildings whose ornamentation consists of great stepped pyramids with false stairways; that is to say, like high towers they flank the real temple but have no functional value. The facades of the temples, both that used as such and those that crown the ornamental pyramids, are decorated with stone mosaic masks, and the tower temples are topped by roof crests. Examples of this style are the cities of Río Bec and Xpuhil.

Chenes contributed to the development of the Puuc style, and typical of both are functional stairways and sloping, stepped bases. The open spaces or doorways are divided by monolithic columns, a feature that appeared perhaps for the first time at Edzná in Campeche. Vertical friezes are richly, even overly, ornamented in busy, but perfectly planned design motifs of huts, panels, latticework, colonnettes, Chaac masks, all in meticulously cut stone mosaic. Here, roof crests rest on the front of the temples. Many cities of Yucatán and Campeche exemplify these styles: Uxmal, Hochob, Edzná, Sayil, Labná, Kabah, etc.

An entire day is needed to visit Uxmal and Kabah with the care they merit. In the first city are some of the most beautiful buildings ever constructed by the Maya. In Kabah, the most notable edifice is the Codz Poop, completely covered with masks of Chaac, the long-nosed rain god. A lovely, unadorned arch signals the beginning of a sacbé, "white road," that connected

Conqueror Francisco Montejo's house on Mérida's main plaza is an extraordinary example of 16th century Plateresque civil architecture. Four warriors stand above the doorway: the lower two dressed in Indian style, the larger upper figures in European armor. *Photo author.*

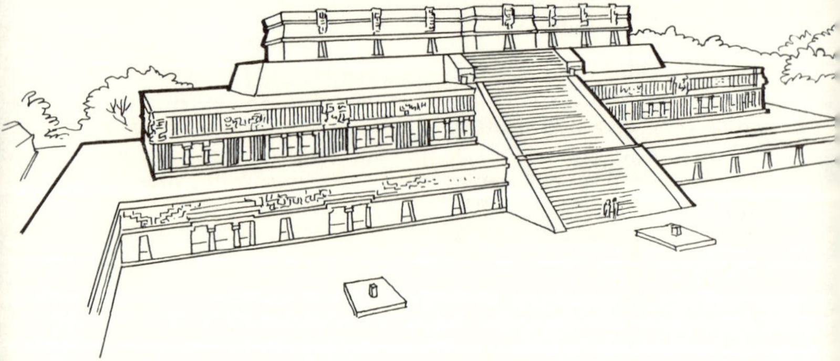

Above, the Palace at Sayil, displaying in its three levels all of the architectural elements of the Puuc-Chenes style.

the two sites, one of a network of limestone-topped roads that once crisscrossed the Peninsula. From Kabah, a new road has provided access to the three small but splendid Maya sites of Sayil, Xlapak and Labná, now all within minutes of each other. The Palace at Sayil and the Arch of Labná are outstanding structures. Fifteen minutes farther along the same road is the entrance to the Caves of Loltún. They are splendidly illuminated, and there is evidence of early Maya occupation.

UXMAL

The harmony, the equilibrium achieved only when the creator spirit is at peace with itself and all its surroundings are evident from the moment the visitor first glimpses Uxmal.

The building immediately visible—the Pyramid of the Magician—sets the mood. It is a monument constructed in several phases, compelling, with the strange enchantment its name implies. The facade faces west, where the sun begins its journey into the world of darkness. Between The Magician and *Kin* (the sun) are more structures, among them the superb Quadrangle of the Nuns. To the north are yet more, but it is to

A section of the Palace of the Governor at Uxmal with its magnificent facade of stone mosaic. *Photo Doris Heyden.*

the south that we find one of the most majestic buildings ever conceived by man, Uxmal's Palace of the Governor.

Splendid, enormously elegant, it is 320 feet long, 40 feet wide and 27 feet high, set on a much larger explanade. The supreme example of Puuc architecture, the Palace, in contrast to the Pyramid of the Magician, faces east, toward the house of the sun. It is divided into three sections by corbeled arches that were once passageways and, later, small sanctuaries.

The lower section of the facade, faced with perfectly mortised stones, is unadorned except for the double frames around the doors and a row of colonnettes along the length of the base. Where Maya imagination reached levels of near obsession is in the marvelous frieze, in the upper section. Thrones, plumed serpents, stepped frets, latticework, columns—the most extraordinary combination of elements—unite to communicate with the viewer in an eloquent, subtle play of light and shadow.

If the visitor senses the esthetic and cultural message of this building, he will have achieved a certain rap-

The Pyramid of the Magician is a complex of structures. Note tunnel entrance in stairway leading to an earlier inner temple with famous "Queen of Uxmal" statue. *Photo Heyden.*

port with the ancient Maya and, with the spiritual gladness thus acquired, will find added delight in his tour of the city. To start, only a few steps behind the Palace, and its eternal companion on the esplanade of the Governor, the House of the Turtles awaits him: tiny, humble, exquisite.

DZIBILCHALTUN

We return to Mérida to take the highway north to the state's most important seaport and beach resort, Progreso. On the way, nine miles from Mérida, is a short paved turnoff to the right leading to the ruins of Dzibilchaltún. First, a visit to the small but well-mounted museum for orientation, then off to tour this large site inhabited from the Late Preclassic (300 B.C. 200 A.D.) to the 16th century. Because it was occupied so long, longer than any other Maya site, Dzibilchaltún has produced a complete ceramic series, representative of all Maya periods.

Of particular interest are the cenote into which offerings were cast to the aquatic gods, and the Temple of the Seven Dolls. This strange, square, windowed structure was so named by archaeologists because here were found seven dolls made of rubber, an offering that shows the Maya knew how to vulcanize rubber. A note of interest is the discovery by investigator Robert Bruce that the Lacandón of Chiapas still fashion dolls of rubber.

From Mérida, a highway to the northwest leads to the port of Sisal. Before the manufacture of plastic fibers, during Yucatán's henequen heyday, it was from this port that the natural fiber was exported; hence the fiber became known as "sisal" rather than "henequen" *(Agave fourcroydes)* on the international market.

Southeast from Mérida is the road to Acanceh and Mayapán. In Acanceh, just off the plaza, lie pyramid remains. From the top, a short distance to the southeast, can be seen a pre-Hispanic structure called the Palace. The top half of the facade is decorated with molded stucco figures placed within a frame. The figures on the bottom row, such as serpent and feline, may relate to the earth, while those in the top band — birds — may refer to the sky.

MAYAPAN

Mayapán reveals the decline and collapse of pre-Hispanic Maya glory, since it was the last of the great Maya cities, founded in the 11th century.

The archaeological zone is immense, and the greater part is surrounded by a wall. Within its confines some

3,500 buildings have been located, mainly civil structures, that were raised around 20 cenotes (no longer functioning). Outstanding among the buildings of Mayapán are the so-called Castillo and El Caracol, similar to those of the same name in Chichén Itzá but in every way inferior, even in size. Noteworthy temples are scarce in Mayapán. In the homes many altars have been found where an ancestral cult was practiced, and some have produced macabre discoveries — skulls covered with a resin that, like a mask, attempted to reconstruct the living features.

Back for an evening in Mérida there is an opportunity to relish the delicious Yucatecan cuisine, dishes like *cochinita pibil,* pit-barbecued pork (p'ib in Maya means "buried"); *huevos a la motuleña,* eggs with everything including ham, fried beans, peas, etc. Deer and pheasant are common items on the menu and while Yucatecan cuisine is generally highly condimented but not hot, it boasts the "bravest" chile in all Mexico, the *habanero.* Chopped together with tomatoes and onions and floated in the juice of the sour orange, it is a side dish at every meal to savor or ignore.

The magnificent archaeological zone of Chichén Itzá is some 75 miles east of Mérida. A short detour from Hoctún on the highway leads to Izamal where an immense 16th-century monastery was built over a pyramid. The cross atop the ancient pyramid of Kinich Kakmo, one of the largest pyramids in Yucatán, is visible driving into Izamal. It is still the focus of pilgrimage, particularly for the Holy Day of the Assumption of the Blessed Virgin, every August 15.

Pisté, a very few kilometers before reaching Chichén, may be regarded as marking the limits between the more or less urban culture to the west, and the rural conservative tradition to the east. The exterior of the old church in Pisté displays carved stones from Chichén Itzá and the baptismal font inside is a re-used pier similar to those at the Temple of the Warriors.

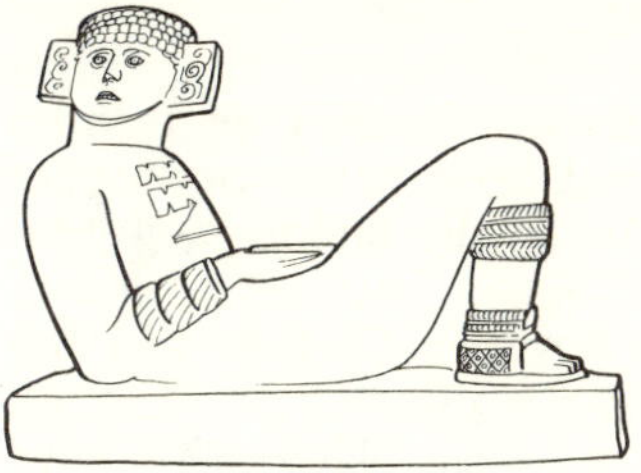

Chac Mol was given that name by French explorer Le Plongeon.* Here, the drawing represents a Maya version of this sculpture from Chichén Itzá now in the National Anthropology Museum, Mexico City.

CHICHEN ITZA

From the soaring, framing arch of the new site museum and tourist center, the monumental Castillo rises high and clear. Also called the Pyramid of Kukulkán, and described by Fray Diego de Landa in the 16th century, there is a more ancient construction in its interior. Archaeologists explored it in such a way that the public has access via a stairway that leads in and up, terminating in the inner temple where two impressive sculptures are on view: a Chac Mol, and a red jaguar with incrustations of green stone. When discovered, the jaguar bore on its back an incomparable mosaic disc of jade and turquoise, later removed for safekeeping.

And to the north, passing the Venus Platform (one of the ancient city's theaters) over what must have been a broad avenue, is the Sacred Well, a heart-stirring sight. The observant visitor will see that the walls of this cenote were probably smoothed by hand.

The Temple of the Warriors and also that of the Jaguars adjoining the Great Ball Court are similar in architecture and motifs to those at the Central Mex-

* It was Auguste Le Plongeon who baptized with the name of Chac Mol a personage of doubtful interpretation, represented as a human figure in a supine position, knees raised. *Chac Mol* is a symbolic name for jaguar, meaning literally "red claw." Le Plongeon arrived in the Maya zone in the 19th century, dynamited the Platform of the Eagles and discovered the sculpture inside. The main purpose of Le Plongeon's "Maya studies" was to prove that the Maya were the creators of Freemasonry.

ican site of Tula. Examples are the serpent column entrance, the human-jaguar-bird-serpent motif, the Chac Mol sculpture, and small anthropomorphic figures.

Breath-taking are the dimensions of the Ball Court, the largest in all Mesoamerica. Although there is no way of knowing whether it was so planned, communication in a normal tone of voice carries across 460 feet from one temple to the other at either extreme of the court.

In the excavated southern part of Chichén Itzá lie buildings which are primarily in the architectural style of Northern Yucatán known as Puuc: El Caracol, doubtless an astronomical observatory; the Church, the Nunnery and its Annex. This is merely an indication; the southern part of the site is for the thoughtful wanderer.

A short distance east of Chichén Itzá a sign marks the entrance road to Balancanché Cave. A chamber, discovered in 1959, had been sealed off a thousand years ago, shortly after offerings were made to the rain god. The ceramic styles and the depicting of the Central Mexican rain god demonstrate familiarity and

The Great Ball Court and associated temples at Chichén Itzá. The Upper Temple of the Jaguars is at the right.

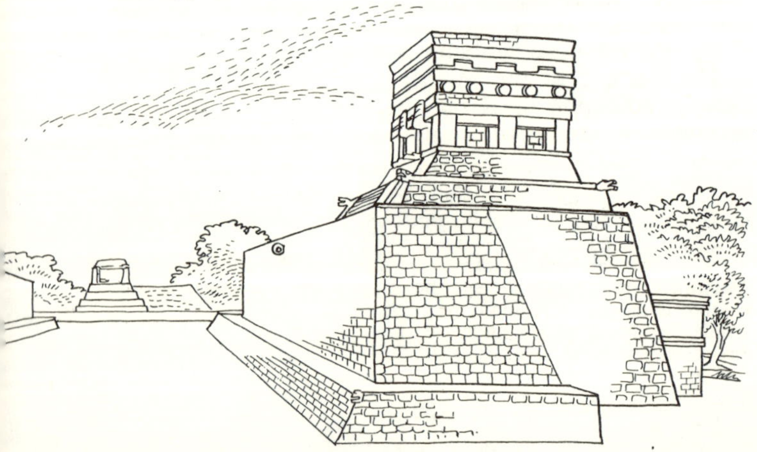

An example of architecture at Chichén Itzá similar to Pyramid B at the Central Mexican site of Tula is the Temple of the Warriors with its immense colonnade.

interaction with people from other areas. Carbon 14 dates from the cave offerings show that this interaction was evident in the area by 900 A.D.

The highway continues through Kaua, Cuncunul and Ebtún, villages that conserve many of the ancient traditions. Houses in ruins testify to the tremendous destruction suffered by the state in the War of Castes.

Valladolid, Yucatán's second city, is next. Several hours can be spent visiting the main church, the 16th-century monastery of San Bernardino, and the enormous Zaci cenote with a small historical museum and a restaurant near its rim. Time out for more of the tasty food of Yucatán: *relleno negro,* black sauce for turkey; chicken pibil; various snacks such as *codzitos, panuchos, papadzules* (regional versions of tacos and enchiladas made with different fillings and sauces), and the spicy sausage for which Valladolid is famous.

Chemax, 18 miles away, is the last town within the state and so conservative that, as late as 1962, life continued as in the pre-Hispanic past. From this point the road leads on to Cancun on the coast of Quintana Roo.

The many small Maya sites along the Caribbean coast of Quintana Roo and on Cancún and the island of Cozumel were founded and flourished as a result of trading activities along the important sea route that

Chichén Itzá: In the foreground is a corner of the upper facade of the "Church," a small building totally covered with carvings. The spiral observatory in the background was probably used as its name implies. *Photo Heyden.*

circumnavigated the Yucatán Peninsula beginning probably in the Late Classic period and continuing in use up to the arrival of the Spaniards. Most of the visible sites, usually unexcavated and unconsolidated, appear to date from the Late Postclassic (1250 A.D. and later).

The best starting point geographically and information-wise is the small but well presented archaeological museum in Cancun, in the Convention Center; maps and publications may be purchased here for future reference. There are remains of Maya buildings at several places on Cancun, some on hotel grounds, even one on the 12th hole of the golf course but the largest and most interesting ruins are those of El Rey in the southern half of the island.

From Cancún it is 42 miles to Playa del Carmen, ferry terminal for the 12-mile crossing to the island of Cozumel. A major stop on the Maya sea trade route, Cozumel has a number of sites and shrines, and was the center of a strong cult to Ix Chel, the moon goddess, patroness of childbirth, procreation, and medicine. More information on the Maya past is to be garnered in the Cozumel archaeological museum.

Along the highway that runs from Cancun to Chetumal are short side roads that lead to the coast and other Postclassic sites: Playa del Carmen, Xcaret, Chakalal, Yalku, Akumal, Xelhá (with submarine Maya structures and beautiful coral formations, lures for snorkeling); Tancah, Chunyaxché, and Muyil.

Tulum, 80 miles south of Cancun, was probably the largest settlement along the Caribbean and is the most extensively excavated and consolidated. It is walled on three sides, with a 40-feet cliff and the sea below as its protection on the fourth. The 16-acre walled section seems to have been ceremonial and residential for an elite, with most of the population living outside the walls. The Temple of the Frescoes has deity representations outlined in black and colored in red, blue and yellow, reminiscent of the Maya codex style. In Maya times most of the buildings were brilliantly painted inside and out.

From Tulum it is a half-hour drive inland to Cobá, an immense site of 81 square miles including four lakes, a rare sight in northern Yucatán. Once a city of at least 50,000 people, it was the hub of many *sacbeob* (white roads) paved in crushed limestone that connected Cobá with other Maya centers. The longest, which averaged 30 feet wide, led 62.3 miles west to Yaxuná, a small site seven miles south of Chichén Itzá. The tallest pyramid in Yucatán is at Cobá, the 120-foot high Nohoch Mul ("Large Hill") and from its summit the whole of the exceedingly flat Yucatán Peninsula seems to be visible.

The causes of the War of Castes in Yucatán:
church domination and
the hacendados' cruel exploitation of the Indian.

WAR OF CASTES

Even though our discussion of the Maya is limited to the highlights, it would not be complete without referring to an event of the past century whose mark is still visible today on two of the largest Maya groups — the Yucatec, and the Tzotzil in the state of Chiapas.

The War of Castes began in Yucatán in 1847 and ended in 1901, when federal troops finally conquered the village of Chan Santa Cruz (now Carrillo Puerto), center of the uprising on the Peninsula. Among the Tzotzil, the rebellion was later in starting (1867) and much briefer, ending in 1871. They were conflicts generated by interethnic relationships resulting in true Indian movements.

In Yucatán, the uprising began on July 20, 1847, as the result of three centuries of almost slave-like exploitation of the natives by their Spanish conquerors. After Independence (1821), the situation became even worse because the slight and fitful protection the Indians had enjoyed directly from the King, through royal limitations imposed upon landholders and provincial authorities, was swept away as the country restructured itself. In desperation, the Indians obtained war materials from the English in Belize and secretly armed themselves. Mexican federal troops were wholly occupied with U.S. expansionist activities on the northern frontier 2,000 miles away.

The first "white" towns to fall were those surrounding the rebel nucleus, located near the border between Quintana Roo and southeastern Yucatán. To the cry of "Death to the Whites," the uprising gathered strength and, as towns fell to the rebels, the horrified inhabitants had to seek refuge in Mérida.

The year 1848 witnessed the near total rout of the whites who, desperate in turn, requested aid from the Mexican government and from the United States.

The U.S. refused; the Mexican government sent troops who, little by little, began to turn the tide. Nevertheless, there was a moment when the only remaining centers of white power on the entire Peninsula were Mérida, some coastal villages, and towns along the Camino Real de Campeche. Mérida was besieged by the Indians who held two-thirds of the Peninsula. But suddenly, as if by magic, the Indians began to leave. And the reason for this phenomenon? The rainy season had started and the Indians were drawn to their villages, to their fields, to the sacred corn!

This allowed the whites to recoup. The Indians began to take refuge in the forests of Quintana Roo, soon filled with rebels. Gradually, the Indians were defeated and forced to withdraw so that, by 1850, they saw their cause—extermination of the whites—as lost. In return for peace, they demanded that they be given, as their autonomous jurisdiction, about the same territory now occupied by the state of Quintana Roo; a demand that was denied.

And then the miracle occurred.

TALKING IDOLS

From pre-Hispanic times, the Maya had developed a cult to a series of deities represented by "talking idols." The most famous of these was on the Island of Cozumel, the object of pilgrimages from all over the Peninsula. Many others were still venerated after the Conquest, like that of Tayasal, worshiped until 1697, year in which the last Maya group was conquered and the idol destroyed by the Indians themselves.

They did not find it strange, therefore, that near the end of 1850 a talking cross should appear in a village later to be called Chan Santa Cruz. It began to speak to them, to raise their spirits, urge them on to war, and to create a new religion, lending a dimension of nativism to what had been a purely political movement. It seems that the creator of this talking cross hoax was a mestizo from Peto, José María Barrera, assisted by

Beside a small cenote near Chan Santa Cruz appeared the first cross in the modern cult of talking crosses. Rude temples were constructed so that the Indians might gather to hear messages delivered by the cruciform oracles.

an Indian ventriloquist named Manuel Nahuat. A new cult rapidly flourished around this mahogany cross.

Unable simply to ignore the phenomenon, the federal government sent troops who made a surprise attack at dawn on March 23, 1851. Barrera managed to escape but Manuel Nahuat was killed in the assault. The cross was destroyed.

Not wishing to remain so far from white-populated areas, the army returned to its main base leaving Chan Santa Cruz unguarded. Barrera thus was able to return unhindered—this time with crosses, in the plural.

A palm-leaf temple was constructed and divided into two sections. In the rear portion three crosses were placed and hailed as "daughters" of the first cross, the Trinity sent from heaven by God the Father. The area occupied by the daughters was called *La Gloria*. Dressed in huipiles, the crosses could be viewed only by their priests, or masters, who spoke from behind them. The priest's voice passed through a barrel so that, when heard by the worshipers at the front of the temple, it had a deep, mysterious resonance.

English army officers, Lieutenants Plumridge and Twigge, who in 1861 went to meet with the Chan Santa Cruz Indians, described the functioning of the temple. They had gone to see the Indian authorities to discuss the problem of incursions into English territory. Received with hostility, they were forced to witness the ceremony of the talking crosses.

At midnight an Indian escort led the British officers to the temple and made them kneel before the altar. The temple was in complete darkness and already filled with Indians praying in silence. . .

"At that moment the soft music and singing that until then had pervaded the building ceased and was followed by a deafening and prolonged sound similar to thunder when heard at a distance. This too ceased, and in the midst of the silence that followed was heard a rather weak voice which seemed to originate in the midst of the air and which spoke the Maya language."

Requests made by the crosses to the fervent Indians were numerous. In response to those daily demands, the masters received money, fowls, corn, whatever they desired.

Native religious zeal—and whips and chains for the uncooperative—resulted in construction by the Indians of a great temple of stone and mortar beginning in 1860. The towers were never built, but the dimensions of the temple were on a monumental scale: 115 feet long, 83 feet wide, and 46 feet high. This temple stands today in the village of Chan Santa Cruz as a silent witness to the cult of the talking cross and to the War of Castes.

Because it was so difficult to pursue the Indians through the jungles of Quintana Roo, the government gradually relinquished possession of the territory to them.

Over a period of time, three independent territorial and political units or *cacicazgos* were formed: Chan Santa Cruz, extending from Bacalar on the south to Tulum on the north; Ixkanha and Chichanha (also called Icaiche), both on the border with the present state of Campeche. Nominally, at least, the latter two signed a peace treaty and surrendered to the government in 1853. For that reason they were called the "peaceful Indian rebels," and for the same reason they were considered traitors and enemies by those of Chan Santa Cruz, the "wild Indian rebels."

Chan Santa Cruz continued to receive arms from Belize, in exchange for allowing the English to exploit the lumber in their territory, and rebels frequently raided other villages in Yucatán. All was now controlled by the Talking Cross, which no longer limited itself to the enrichment of its masters, but decided all matters relating to the cacicazgo, political as well as religious.

To carry out their plans, the priests formed a triumvirate: the Patron of the Cross or *tatich,* highest authority and true Cacique; the Interpreter of the Cross or *tata polin;* and the Commander of the Plaza, who was described as being "under the orders of the tatich and subject to the same punishment as anyone else."

One of the tatich's officers was a spy to avoid, on one hand, a coup d'etat by the other members of the triumvirate and, on the other, to inform on activities throughout the Peninsula, thus aiding in making decisions on military strategy.

An observer of the period described the whole system vividly:

"The manner in which these Indians meet to hear the divine word is as follows: Always in the afternoon the people unexpectedly hear the prophetic note of a trumpet which announces one of these supposed interviews between God and the triumvirate. The populace becomes disturbed and agitated. God is going to descend! At nightfall the three priests take their posts in a sort of open cabinet in the wall.

Outside and around the temple the people wait, frightened and expectant . . . At eight in the evening, bells ring, and all the trumpets of the military band sound. God has descended! Awe maintains profound silence, broken a few moments later by mysterious trumpets which call for attention. Only the indefinable murmur of a thousand respirations and animals moving in the brush are heard. Then a sharp and ugly sound. This is the whistle of the Organ of the Divine Word, an artifice simulating the voice of divinity. Interrogation by the three impostors begins, and at the end they come from the temple and communicate the sentence of God to the people."

Living descendants of those Indians still preserve manuscripts of some of the messages. One of them, collected by Villa Rojas in X-Cacal, will serve as an example of how the Talking Cross governed its subjects:

"So, therefore, my dear Christians, I command all of you, great and small, know you that now has arrived the day and the year in which my Indians shall once more rise up against the whites . . . that however much they hear and observe the firing upon them from the rifles of the whites, to none shall there be done any hurt, for already have arrived the hour and the day in which my native Indians again enter into combat against the whites, as when there was fighting of old; for ye must know, O Christian folk, that I shall always be with you in all times; I shall always be he that goeth before you in the vanguard, confronting the enemy, so that no harm may befall you, my dear Indians."*

The War of Castes in Yucatán ended in 1901, but much that came out of it, both civil and religious, persisted into the 1940's. Then for a time little was heard, but lately many Indians have returned to the jungle and are reviving old traditions, as I have mentioned.

---

* Some data for this chapter and the three extracts quoted above were taken from *The Maya of East Central Quintana Roo,* by Alfonso Villa Rojas (1961).

Let us now examine how the War of Castes developed among the Tzotzil of Chiapas, and how it is reflected in some of their present-day customs.

Many Tzotzil villages participated in the 1867-71 war, but none to the extent of San Juan Chamula, focal point of activity throughout the entire period.

On December 22, 1867, a young Indian shepherdess, Agustina Gómez Checheb, alleged to have seen three stones fall from heaven as she tended her flock. She took the stones home where they remained until January 10, 1868, when Pedro Díaz Cuscat, as fiscal (a minor lay office of the church), went to investigate the "miracle" of the stones which, by then, had acquired certain fame. But instead of delivering the stones to the parish priest, Díaz Cuscat took them to his home and placed them in a box. He then began to convince his neighbors that the stones "knocked on the lid to get out," and that they were objects of worship.

Soon the Indians began to take offerings to the stones, and Díaz Cuscat, with the aid of Agustina Gómez Checheb, caused the stones "to speak" to those who worshiped them. Later, clay figures were added to the sacred stones. Díaz Cuscat declared that Agustina had given birth to them and, therefore, should be called "Mother of God."

Díaz Cuscat named as his advisors men who could read and write, and who prepared for him a list of all the villages and ranches where Tzotzils lived or worked. He assigned a patron saint to each village, and encouraged the cult to the stones and figurines.

Later he began to preach to the Indians that they should not continue worshiping the saints of the *ladinos* (whites), but that they should acquire their own saint by crucifying some member of the group who would then serve as their messiah.

On Good Friday, 1868, a boy 10 or 11 years old, Domingo Gómez Checheb, was crucified, the blood removed from his body and perfumed with incense. An author of that period even suggests that the blood was drunk by the leaders of the movement. It is not known what exactly was the relationship between Domingo and Agustina, but it is curious that they should bear the same surname—the child selected to die on the cross, and the Mother of God. The child's parents were identified by chroniclers of the time as Juan Gómez Checheb and Manuela Pérez Jolcogtom.

Inhabitants of the "white" town of San Cristóbal Las Casas began to realize that something was happening in neighboring San Juan Chamula when, during Lent of 1868, not one Indian appeared to worship at the image of the Burial of Christ in the Church of Santo Domingo, a pilgrimage center of long standing. Obviously, the cult to the Passion of the Indian child had replaced that to the Passion of Christ.

A few months later, in the Indian zone, great preparations were made to celebrate the fiesta of Santa Rosa on August 30, 1868. Díaz Cuscat ordered that the house of the saint be repaired and that neighboring villages be invited. Together with other prominent personages, he hastened to appoint sacristans, acolytes and a majordomo. In this way, the lay offices in the church that had always been held by Indians became part of the new Indian cult. Díaz Cuscat had a white robe made for himself, like those worn by Catholic priests, and Agustina Gómez Checheb, now called Santa Luisa, was dressed in a special outfit embroidered in silk. Thus, Díaz Cuscat promoted himself from fiscal to priest.

The parish priest of Chamula was not ignorant of what was going on. Aided by the political boss of San Cristóbal Las Casas, he did everything possible to prevent the Indians from meeting together, and even managed the arrest of Agustina, Díaz Cuscat, and Manuela Pérez Jolcogtom, mother of the Indian savior. The three were jailed in December 1868 in San Cristóbal.

During the following months nothing happened until, just as in Yucatán, a *ladino* or mestizo, took over the movement. Professor Ignacio Fernández de Galindo, born in Mexico City but residing in San Cristobal, and probably aware of the rebellion in Yucatán, carried the Chamula uprising on into its military phase.

Ignacio Fernández de Galindo operated a secondary school in San Cristóbal which was considered too "progressive" by the reactionary society of that city. On May 17, 1869, during a public examination in which Galindo was questioning his most brilliant student, he got into a heated argument with Fernando Zepeda, editor of two conservative newspapers. Galindo won the discussion from the "scientific" point of view but Zepeda, through his tremendous political influence, induced the students to desert the school. Galindo decided to avenge himself on the people who had humiliated him and, together with his wife, Luisa Quevedo, and a faithful student, Benigno Trejo, he went on horseback to San Juan Chamula.

Upon reaching the village, Galindo immediately sought out the house of Díaz Cuscat's relatives. Telling them he was a messenger from Díaz Cuscat and was going to direct the movement to free him, Galindo persuaded the family to let him have the figures.

As proof of his good faith, he and his companions dressed themselves as Indians. From that moment he began to fan the hatred of the Indians against the whites, and to prepare his followers militarily. When he felt that his "troops" were ready, he decided to attack San Cristóbal Las Casas. That decision was speeded up when, on June 11, 1869, in Galindo's absence, the parish priest entered his house and removed the box with the clay figures. When Galindo discovered the theft, his fury was such that, together with Trejo and some Indians, he murdered the priest.

Then the newspapers of San Cristóbal finally began to concern themselves with events. Army troops were requested to put down the uprising, but they were late in coming. A small defensive force was raised among the inhabitants of San Cristóbal. Siege of the city began on June 17, 1869, when the Indians arrived armed with a few shotguns, knives, pointed sticks and lances. Galindo could be recognized easily because he was wearing a monkey-skin hat with a red ribbon, as befitted the Commander-in-Chief.

When the commander of the white troops came out to face the Indians, something unexpected happened: Galindo appeared, bearing a white flag, and offered himself, his wife and his disciple in exchange for the liberty of Díaz Cuscat and Agustina Gómez Checheb. The proposal was accepted and the two Indian martyrs returned to San Juan Chamula to assume leadership of the rebellion.

Galindo counted upon being liberated from his jail cell by a grateful Díaz Cuscat. Three days later, however, when the Indians returned to San Cristóbal and demanded Galindo's release, the state reinforcements had arrived and the request was denied. In the ensuing battle 300 Indians and a few whites were killed. Galindo and Trejo were executed on June 26th, accused of being traitors to their class.

After other encounters, the Indians took up strategic positions in the mountains, the ladinos in the valley. From their bastions the Indians made forays on towns and ranches where they killed everyone, including women and children. The movement began to lose force around 1870—no decisive battle terminated the war. There was still talk of Indian uprisings in 1871, but nothing happened.

The War of Castes left a deep mark on San Juan Chamula: no Catholic priest has ever returned to live there; a new cult to an Indian Christ was instituted; new religious posts were created; and still today, during Carnival, San Juan Chamula's principal fiesta, reminders of the War of Castes are in evidence. Beginning after the French Intervention and the brief empire of Maximilian and Carlota (1861-67), the War of Castes coincided with a frontier dispute with Guatemala. During Carnival the three events are merged into one.

Of the many rites and events staged from Carnival

to Holy Week that are reminders of that period, I shall mention only two.

DURING HOLY WEEK

In two other villages that participated in the War of Castes, San Pedro Chenalhó and Zinacantan, images called The Nazarene and The Burial of Christ, respectively, are worshiped. Only in San Juan Chamula, mother of the rebellion, does worship center almost exclusively around an Indian who personifies Christ: *El Pasión* (The Passion).

Fiesta activities are organized by former Pasiones who have had outstanding success. They indicate when and how rites should be carried out and even perform some. In reality, the religion and its functioning are in the hands of these counselors. El Pasión must personally assume the expenses of the festivities (about 800 dollars) and he is accompanied by his wife, who reincarnates Agustina Gómez Checheb.

Many of the acts are reminiscent of the Catholic Passion drama, even though the Christ worshiped is not the Catholic one. For example, the Pasiones and their helpers make pilgrimages to the various calvaries or sanctuaries of the Cross in San Juan Chamula. And on Good Friday, they erect a cross to which they tie an image of Christ.

There is another cult, however, that exists in Chamula together with that of El Pasión: the traditional veneration of the Catholic saints, whose images are housed in the town's main church. In this cult, too, many ancient rites are mixed. The result is what I believe to be a new and different religion, tinged with ancient Maya tradition.

CARNIVAL FESTIVITIES

The other event I wish to mention is a burlesque battle on the last day of Carnival week. The actors wear uniforms patterned after those of the French grenadiers who came to Mexico during the Intervention. They also wear monkey-skin caps, reminiscent both of

Tzotzils running across fire in another of the Carnival ceremonies at San Juan Chamula. Of pre-Hispanic origin, it is, without doubt, a purification rite.

the one used by Galindo, and of the French kepi. As if they were soldiers, they refer to each other as "Captain" and "General." Due to the hat, they are known as "monkeys," *mashetik.*

The monkeys are divided into two groups, one located at the foot of a nearby hill, and the other higher up, recalling the positions of the white forces in the valley and the Indian forces on the mountainside. One group represents Mexico; the other, Guatemala.

During the battle they attack each other, throwing balls of manure. When an Indian was asked why, he answered: "Because if they threw stones they could hurt each other." In the first battle, Mexico loses. In the second, Guatemala loses, and the third is a draw.

This encounter ends the most significant fiesta of a very conservative contemporary Maya group, the Tzotzil, who have integrated their history into their celebrations, and continue to maintain a hostile attitude toward the whites.

THE ANCIENT MAYA

Before going on to the last half of this book, I would like to make an observation. As the reader will have noted, the text has not been organized chronologically from the remote past down to the present. Rather, I felt it would be better to begin by describing the contemporary Maya, trace the course of their pre-Hispanic glory, and conclude with the happening that produced the synthesis of the two periods, bringing to a close the past and foreshadowing the future: the Conquest by Spain.

The brief account of the Ancient Maya that follows is based on what has gone before. To avoid a twice-told tale, the reader must keep this in mind if he is to understand some of the descriptions to come. Now, let us start on our fabulous journey into Maya antiquity . . .

"This is the account of how all was in suspense, all at peace, in silence, immobile, quiet and empty the expanse of the heavens.

"This is the first account, the first discourse. There was not yet a man neither were there animals, birds, fish, crabs, trees, stones, caves, canyons, plants nor forests, only the sky existed.

"The face of the earth was not in evidence. There was only the calm sea, and the sky in all of its extension.

"There was nothing standing; only the water in repose, the peaceful sea, alone and tranquil. Nothing had been given life.

"There was only immobility and silence in the darkness, in the night. Only the Creator, the Maker, Tepeu, Gucumatz, the Forefathers, were in the water surrounded by clarity... Great sages, great thinkers they are by nature. In this way the heavens existed and also the *Corazón del Cielo* (Heart of Heaven), this being the name of God and this is how he is called.

"The word then reached here; together came Tepeu and Gucumatz, in the darkness, in the night, and Tepeu and Gucumatz talked between themselves. They spoke to each other then, consulting and meditating; they came to agreement, joined their words and thought.

"Then it became clear, as they meditated, that when dawn came, man should appear... Let it be done thusly. Let the emptiness be filled. Let this water withdraw and vacate (space). Let the land surge upward and it shall be solid. So they spoke. Let there be light, let there be dawn in the heavens and on earth. There will be neither glory nor grandeur in our creation and making until the human creature exists, man formed. Thus they spoke."

In this poetic form, magnificently, the Maya-Quiché of Guatemala recorded the divine decision to create man, in one of the most extraordinary books ever written: the *Popol Vuh.* To piece together the millennial history of the ancient Maya, however, the scientist must look elsewhere for more factual information.

THE PROTO-MAYA

We have already seen that a proto-Maya community probably existed in northwest Guatemala around 2600 B.C. But that group was not, of course, the creator of the material remains of the culture that we can assign to the ethnic ancestors of the present Mayance groups. Most investigators now agree that the most ancient of these remains date from much later, as late as around 500 B.C. What was happening during all the intervening time?

Centuries passed as gradually that proto-community subdivided and migrations began that were to result in the different Maya groups and their respective languages. Migrations not only separated the groups, but also allowed cultural contacts to be established with other groups that had reached their full development or were well on their way. Those contacts have given rise to the differences of opinion among specialists with respect to the place in which the true Maya was born and began to develop.

Some insist that Maya origins were in southern Veracruz-northern Tabasco where, more than ten centuries before Christ, a local culture known as Olmec began to develop and disseminate its influence throughout most of Mesoamerica, including the Maya area.

Others believe, as I do, that the true Maya began in the Guatemala highlands. This is not to deny, however, the obvious influences they received from other groups among which, at the beginning, the Olmec was pre-eminent. From the Olmec, the Maya inherited certain technology; some architectural elements; and most important of all, a rudimentary numeric and calendaric system, based on a vigesimal sequence that allowed the Maya to elaborate through their own efforts, one of the most exact calendars ever devised.

Some of the traits that define the Classic Maya — stelae and Long Count dates, are documented earliest in the highlands. But other characteristics of the Classic Maya, the corbeled vault and architectural iconography, are found to date, earlier in the lowland. A combination of elements from both highland and lowland came to define the people we know as the Classic Maya and were in place in the lowlands by the second century A. D.

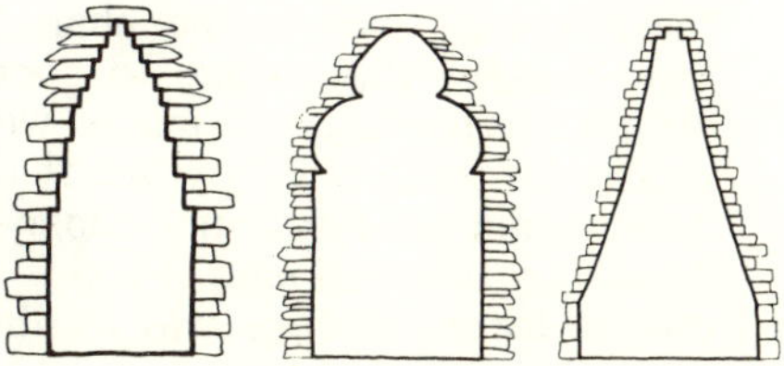

The corbeled vault takes many forms; three are shown. It is not a true arch since it was not completed with a keystone but roofed over.

HISTORICAL PERIODS

A general chronology of Maya history is presented below:

Preclassic (1500 B.C. - 200 A.D.)	
Early	1500 - 900 B.C.
Middle	900 - 300 B.C.
Late	300 B.C. - 200 A.D.
Classic (200 - 1000 A.D.)	
Early	200 - 500 A.D.
Middle	500 - 600 A.D.
Late	600 - 1000 A.D.
Postclassic (1000 - 1600 A.D.)	
Early	1000 - 1250 A.D.
Late	1250 - 1600 A.D.

The *Preclassic* period was a time of transformation from egalitarian farming communities to social, political and economic structures of increasing complexity. Intensive agricultural methods and water control made their appearance in the Middle Preclassic but it is in the Late Preclassic that many of the characteristics we identify as Maya crystallize, such as the stela-altar sculptural ensemble, and hieroglyphic recording. Villages swelled as population increased; small, impermanent structures were replaced with monumental, stucco decorated civic buildings.

Pottery was of good quality though simple in form, and there appeared a cult to handmade clay figurines, representing nude persons chiefly, although on occasion they wore clothing, earplugs and necklaces. Frequently they reveal the typical cranial deformation of the Maya, as well as the characteristic aquiline nose. Graves show that access to goods was unequal, with wealth concentrated probably within one lineage.

The large, stepped pyramids decorated with stucco masks built at this time display a new imagery emphasizing the Sun and Venus. The control of these cosmic forces in time was attributed to one man, the king, who wore their symbols as part of his ceremonial dress.

Despite space limitation, I cannot forego a description of pyramid E-VII-sub in the Petén city of Uaxactún, some miles north of Tikal and belonging to this Preclassic period. The designation given to the pyramid by archaeologists tells us something about Maya customs. For example, after a certain period of time Maya pyramids, even though in perfect repair, were covered successively by others. To discover the earliest, archaeologists must tunnel in from the outermost wall to the center. Thus, along the extension of the exploratory tunnel appear the interior walls of one structure hard up against the exterior walls of the previous edifice.

E-VII-sub of Uaxactún was under a later pyramid —in such an advanced state of ruination that it could not be reconstructed—therefore, "sub." Also, it was mound No. VII of group E, number and letter that indicate the immensity of Maya cities in general.

Finished with a layer of white stucco, the pyramid had a stairway up each side, flanked by huge jaguar masks, a clear indication of Olmec influence. The jaguar, evidently held sacred, was so frequently used as an art motif that it unmistakably identifies the typically Olmec. Although stylized, this element is prominent in pyramid E-VII-sub.

Post holes were found atop the pyramid, indicating the temple that crowned it was of hut construction, perhaps with a palm roof and other features of the huts which, in that epoch of the Preclassic, were practically the same as those built by the Maya today.

Eric Thompson has given us an eloquent description of this impression upon seeing E-VII-sub for the first time:

"We visited this group after dinner on the evening following our arrival. From where we stood on the summit of a pyramid at the end of the group, the plaza below, crisscrossed with trenches dug to trace floor levels and in search of potsherds

Pyramid E-VII-sub of Uaxactún displays evidence of archaic influences on Maya art; in this case, Olmec. Covered with stucco, the pyramid has a stairway on each side.

of stratigraphical significance, looked like a miniature battle-field, but the stucco-covered pyramid beyond, softened by the light of a full moon, was indescribably beautiful. Behind it the forest, spared at the time the ruins were cleared of vegetation, supplied a curtain of velvet black, enhancing the cream-white of the stucco. Even the grotesque features of the huge stucco masks were converted into reposeful beauty by the magic touch of moonlight.

"At the foot of the pyramid stood a weathered stela, the carved surface of which, gray with age, recorded its erection over fourteen centuries ago. It bore the date 9.3.0.0.0. 2 Ahau 18 Muan, January 28, A.D. 495, and almost certainly had been placed in position when the later E-VII pyramid was erected (the hole for the butt cut through earlier floors). Providing the stela had not been moved from some other position—and that is quite an assumption, since the Maya moved stelae around—the later building is dated by the stela, and the earlier pyramid was earlier still. Stylistically it appears to be a lot earlier."*

* From *Maya Archaeologist* by J. Eric S. Thompson. Copy-right 1963 by the University of Oklahoma Press.

Very little must now remain of this marvel that, after its exploration, was again abandoned to the jungle.

The *Classic Period* is subdivided into three eras. By the *Early* appeared two elements of great importance that were to survive for many centuries: typically Maya architecture with the false arch, or roofing with the corbeled vault; and the inception of the stelae cult (dates were carved on the stelae) or the cult to time. All this occurred at the beginning of the Early era, so that two centuries later many Maya cities were erecting numerous hieroglyphic monuments. Maya art evolved its characteristic elements and, at the same time, all the elements of non-Maya influences in the Pre-classic disappeared.

The *Classic* period was the greatest in sculpture, hieroglyphic writing, and construction in the lowlands, with the rise of cities like Tikal, Copán, Quiriguá, Bonampak, Yaxchilán, and Palenque. As never before or after, the Maya perfected their skills in lapidary, figure-making, and magnificently painted ceramics, while at the same time making their greatest strides in astronomy and advanced mathematics. This is the era in which the greatest number of ceremonial· centers erected stelae. For example, in 19 cities hieroglyphic monuments have been found dedicated to the year 790 A.D.

The Classic came to an end in 1000 A.D. Little by little, the great ceremonial centers were abandoned (although not entirely in the lowlands, as we saw in the chapter on the Lacandón); the influences of foreign peoples, perhaps the cause of this collapse, reached the area. They so affected the cities of the Puuc region (Uxmal, Sayil, Labná, Kabah, etc.) that many were deserted by the end of this period or later.

THEORY TO EXPLAIN COLLAPSE

Early in the book I spoke of a theory that, much more realistically than ideas advanced previously, attempts to account for the collapse of many Classic cities — extension of the Mexican* influence to the Maya area, in the beginning transmitted to them by other Maya groups. It is the theory of the late authority Eric Thompson, and can be explained as follows:

In the section on Maya languages, mention was made of Chontal (B-1). The word *chontal* is not Maya, but comes from the Nahuatl *chontalli,* meaning "foreigner," by which Mexican neighbors of the Maya designated three, or perhaps four, distinct Maya linguistic groups. Some of those Maya groups referred to themselves as Putún.

At the moment of the Spanish Conquest, Putún territory extended over much of the Peninsula. Mexican peoples settled on the border of the Maya area mixed with the Putún in the delta region of the Grijalva river.

This immense territory is covered by a network of creeks, rivers, lagoons, swamps and, in the past as now, water was the preferred form of transportation. The Putún thus became great navigators and merchants. Their Mexican neighbors were also merchants but not navigators. When they reached the Putún frontier they were obliged to entrust their cargoes to the Putún, who transported them over a water route they controlled. This route circled the Yucatán Peninsula from the Laguna de Términos to the Sula Plain in Honduras with many ports of call along the way.

Based on the foregoing, and summarizing Thompson's hypothesis: The Putún were influenced by their

---

* A note as to the meaning of the term "Mexican" when it is used in this book. A culture known as Nahua was spread throughout Mesoamerica by groups from the Mexican central highlands beginning perhaps at least as far back as the Classic period of Teotihuacan (300 - 600 A.D.).

The Nahuatl language may have been spoken by the Toltecs, after the fall of Teotihuacan, and it was later the tongue of the Aztecs, who called themselves Mexica (meh-she-kah) or Mexicans. By extension, everything Nahuatl is herein referred to as Mexican.

With Teotihuacan, then, Mexican influence among the Maya began, a very clear influence that appeared in cities as far removed as Tikal and Kaminaljuyú in Guatemala.

Mexican neighbors. By maintaining the maritime routes around Yucatán, they were able to control a series of ports, and even to establish a beachhead at Polé on the east coast. From Polé they penetrated deeper into the mainland and took or became allied with various towns, including Chichén which then acquired the name of the Putún branch that conquered it, the Itzá. This may have occurred as early as the ninth or as late as the tenth century.

Around 800 A.D. still other Putún peoples had established a trading base in Altar de Sacrificios, at the confluence of the Pasión and Chixoy rivers. From Altar de Sacrificios, about 850 A.D., the Putún moved on to conquer Seibal, an important Late Classic city, where they left numerous remains that clearly demonstrate Mexican influences. Later, the Putún advanced still further to Ucanal on the border of what is now Belize, in the Belize river basin.

During the *Late Classic* there is evidence of other Putún-Maya interaction at various sites in Yucatán, including that which took place at Chichén Itzá, for several centuries the dominant city in Yucatán. From the ninth to the 13th century, when Putún groups expanded their maritime activities, thanks to their large seagoing canoes, the resulting commerce enabled Yucatán to develop economically and politically. These Putún may have been allied with other peoples, such as the Toltecs of Tula in Central Mexico, accounting for the shared style and iconography at both sites. (The style associated with Central Mexican models is generally alluded to under the rubric of "Toltec" but such elements appear in the Maya archaeological record as early as the eighth century — earlier than the present accepted dates for the Toltecs of Tula.)

After the collapse of many Classic cities and the fall of the nobility, all induced by them as they Mexicanized the Classic Maya world, the Putún settled south of the Pasión river and called their land Acalan, a Nahuatl word meaning "place of the canoes" or "of

Fragment of a mural found in Chichén Itzá showing life in a fishing village. According to Eric Thompson, neither the figures nor the objects are typical of the Maya art of the Chichén region, and he believes it is a Putún village depicted by the Putún invaders of Chichén.

the canoe people," in memory of Acala, their land of origin south and east of Laguna de Términos.

In that second Acala they remained independent until 1695 when they were conquered by the Spaniards and their principal city was prophetically renamed "Dolores" (pains).

CHICHEN AND THE ITZA

Chichén Itzá means "in the mouth of the well of the Itzá," but the precise significance of *Itzá* is not known. Ralph Roys thought it was the name of a plant or tree, and Barrera Vázquez translates it as "sorcerer of the water."

Who were the Itzá? We have already seen that Thompson thinks they were Mexicanized Maya groups. The fact that they are characterized as speaking broken Maya supports the thesis that they were Putún Maya, not Mexicans introduced into the land of the Maya, as some authorities have suggested.

According to the Chilam Balam of Chumayel, about 1000 A.D. the chiefs of Chichén Itzá felt the need to form an alliance with the Cocom of Mayapán and the Xiu of Uxmal. Both the Xiu and the Cocom claimed to be descendants of the Mexicans. The Xiu boasted of having built the beautiful city of Uxmal but everything indicates they arrived after the city had been abandoned by its true builders.

The alliance was broken in 1194 by Hunac Ceel, leader of the Cocom of Mayapán. Hostilities resulted in the defeat of the Itzá. The ruling families of both Chichén Itzá and Uxmal were carried off to Mayapán from whence they "governed" through delegates.

After the subjection of Chichén by the Cocom, the city was gradually abandoned and no important monument was constructed after that date. Its inhabitants concerned themselves only with making the most necessary repairs, often utilizing materials from buildings that had already fallen into ruins.

In 1533 the Spaniards occupied the city and for three centuries thereafter little was reported. John L. Stephens described his stay there in 1842 while his companion Frederick Catherwood recorded the buildings still standing in detailed drawings. Desiré Charnay published a report of his journey there in 1885 in a work on his Mexican travels and, while Le Plongeon attempted to explore in the area during 1873-74, it was not until 1894 when Edward Thompson, then U.S. Consul in Yucatán, bought the Hacienda Chichén (including the ruins) that organized exploration was undertaken. With funds from the Peabody Museum at

Chichén Itzá's Sacred Well, with remains of buildings on the rim. The walls appear to have been smoothed by hand.

Harvard, he started to investigate the Sacred Well. He wished to prove the tradition of human sacrifices in the well, and to bring up the offerings cast into its depths. To that end, he learned to dive under the tutelage of a Greek diver. Explorations were carried out from 1904 to 1907.

Then, beginning in 1923, for a period of 18 years the Mexican Anthropology Department and the Carnegie Institution of Washington jointly conducted a scientific exploration of the immense site under the direction of José Reygadas Vértiz and Sylvanus F. Morley. In 1960-61 the Well was again explored and, with new techniques, many offerings that had escaped Edward Thompson were recovered.

WAR AND DECLINE

The biggest break in continuity in the Maya world came not with the Mexicanized Putún and the elements they introduced into Maya art and architecture in the

Late Classic, but in the Late Postclassic with the rise of Mayapán and a decisive decline in the quality of artistic expression.

Mayapán became supreme, establishing an "empire" on the Peninsula in the Late Postclassic. Similar action was taken by the Quiché Maya in the Guatemala highlands, but in the 14th century a series of uprisings began against both the Quiché and Mayapán.

Mayapán's supremacy ended in 1441 when a Xiu chief of Uxmal named Ah Xupan Xiu, backed by other chiefs, destroyed the city and left it deserted. The entire Cocom family was massacred, with the exception of one prince who happened to be away on a trading expedition to Honduras. The Quiché divided up into small chieftainships and lived in a state of constant hostility.

The Spanish Conquest of Guatemala was effected in 1525, and of Yucatán in 1541, although the Putún Maya remained independent in Acalan until 1695 and the Itzá in Tayasal until 1697. So ended the history of the pre-Hispanic Maya, and the vicissitudes of their direct descendants began.

Mayapán pottery, from the Late Postclassic period of Maya art. The hooknosed god carries a jar in one hand, and a ball of flaming copal in the other.

MATHEMATICS AND CALENDAR SYSTEM

The reader may skip over this chapter, simply accepting the fact that the Maya are considered mathematical geniuses. But, if so, he will fail to understand clearly why they are so described, as well as miss a salubrious mental exercise.

Eric Thompson says that if the Maya of the Classic period had held a conversation with Classic-period Greeks it would have been carried out with great dignity and mutual understanding of similar complicated social systems, moral principles, religions with a complex pantheon, and extraordinary cosmologies. But if the Maya had attempted to discuss their philosophy of time with the Greeks, he adds, they would have encountered a total lack of comprehension. Thompson is right. No people in the history of humanity has pondered so much on time as the Maya. Their philosophy is unique.

The Maya of the Classic period believed that cycles repeat themselves. They created a system they felt gave them certain control over the nature of those cycles; but when cycles were frankly ominous, when they had a negative sign, the Maya simply resigned themselves because they thought all was possible except to defy the will of the gods. Thus they integrated their existence into the cosmos: Time was God and God was Time.

SOLAR AND RITUAL CALENDARS

In general, all the Mesoamerican peoples had a solar and a ritual calendar. Among the Maya, the ritual calendar that served to fix the dates of fiestas honoring the gods and, at the same time, predict the destinies of individuals according to their birth date, was called *Tzolkin*. The calendar to record the solar year was called *Haab*. (This latter name is used for convenience, but there is no assurance that it was the term actually employed by the Classic Maya).

Stela B of Copán, bearing date glyphs corresponding to 732 A.D. It was in the city of Copán that Maya sculptors gave their reliefs an almost third-dimensional character, as with this richly-garbed dignitary surrounded by symbols and god representations, who seems about to step down from the stela. *Photo Doris Heyden*

The solar calendar was measured in cycles, but cycles of 52, rather than 100, years. That 52-year period of 18,980 days (52×365) is called a Calendar Round.

In fact, the Maya believed the year to have 365 and a fraction days, their figure being closer to the duration of the tropical year than that assigned to it by our Gregorian calendar. A comparative table published years ago by John E. Teeple illustrates this extraordinary intellectual achievement:

Present duration of year	365.2422 days
Duration of year around 600 A.D.	365.2423
Julian year	365.2500
Gregorian year	365.2425
Maya year in Copán	365.2420

Teeple makes special mention of the Maya year in Copán, for it appears that such impressive exactitude

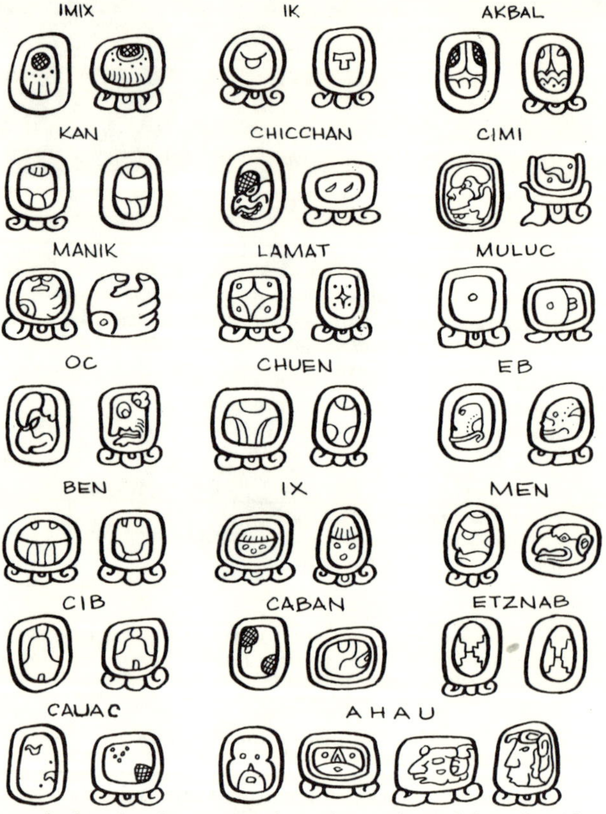

Day glyphs, showing two variants for each, and four for Ahau, indicating the many there are for that day.

was achieved in that city around 600 A.D., and remained in effect during the rest of the Classic period.

The Maya also achieved the permutation or intercalation of three cycles in one. The Tzolkin used 20 days, each with its name. Those 20 day-names were counted from 1 to 13 so that upon reaching the 14th day, that day-name became No. 1 and the day-name that had figured as No. 1 in the first round became No. 8 in the second, and did not appear again as No. 1 until after

While the day glyphs, opposite, were used in the Tzolkin calendar, month glyphs, above, corresponded to the Haab.

13 rounds. This system, therefore, incorporates two cycles, one that goes from 1 to 13 and the other from 1 to 20, whose permutation allows a total of 260 combinations of numbers and names of days ($13 \times 20 = 260$). And that was the Tzolkin, a ritual calendar of 260 days.

The Haab or solar calendar also had 20 days, but those days were designated by number, 0 to 19, grouped in 18 months, each with a name, to which were added 5 days called *uayeb* ($20 \times 18 + 5 = 365$).

4 AHAU 8 CUMKU

Names and glyphs of the Maya days and months appear in the two illustrations, making the meaning of a date clear. In accordance with the foregoing, if today's date is 4 Ahau 8 Cumku (4 Ahau being the day of the Tzolkin and 8 Cumku being the 8th day of the month Cumku in the Haab), 52 years, or 18,980 days, will have to pass before the same combination recurs.

How did the Maya combine their two calendars so that in stating a date they cited those of both the Tzolkin and the Haab? How had they managed the permutation or intercalation of the two calendars?

The answer to this seemingly very difficult problem demonstrates once again the genius of that marvelous people, and was based on a simple mathematical permutation. They found the factor or common divisor. Both 260 and 365 are divisible by 5, so by multiplying 5×52 (cycles of 365 days)×73 (cycles of 260 days) they again obtained 18,980 days, resulting in combined calculations of the two calendars with absolute precision within a 52-year cycle.

But the Maya were not satisfied with this. They invented a system that allowed them to make perfect calculations for much longer periods. They were able to calculate, without error, periods of up to 90 million years. We know this system under the name of Initial Series or Long Count.

NUMBERS AND SYSTEMS

To explain it, let us start with a few generalities. A millennium before any other culture in the world, some Mesoamerican peoples (the first appear to have been the Olmec) invented relative numerical positioning; that is, they gave value to numbers according to the position they occupied. The Maya carried this system to its ultimate perfection using, for the first time, the concept of zero.

The basis of their mathematical succession was not the decimal system we use, but the vigesimal.

Basically, we have 10 ideograms or mathematical symbols, from 1 to 9 and 0. The Romans also had various ideograms: I, X, L, C, etc. But the Romans found themselves in problems we do not have. For example, 19 for them was an X plus IX, and the latter, at the same time, was a subtraction, 10 minus 1.

We, like the Maya, however, give value to numbers in accordance with their position, placing them one next to the other in a horizontal line, reading them from left to right.

In the first position, on the left, we cannot go farther than 9 because to arrive at tens, the basis of our mathematical succession, we have to pass to the following position. That is, to pass from one position to the following, we must always multiply by 10.

The same occurred in the Maya system, except that they multiplied by 20 and the positions were registered vertically, in the following way:

5th position:	8,000	twenties	(160,000)
4th position:	400	twenties	(8,000)
3rd position:	20	twenties	(400)
2nd position:		twenties	(20)
1st position:		units	(1)

And thus successively, always multiplying by 20. The Maya also had ideograms or "numbers," but basically there were only three: the dot with a value of 1; the bar with a value of 5, and a kind of stylized conch shell for zero. (See the accompanying illustration showing all the combinations from zero to 19.)

In the first position, therefore, while we can write symbols from 1 to 9 only, the Maya wrote from 1 to 19. If they wished to write 20, they put a dot in the second position and a zero in the first. If they placed a dot

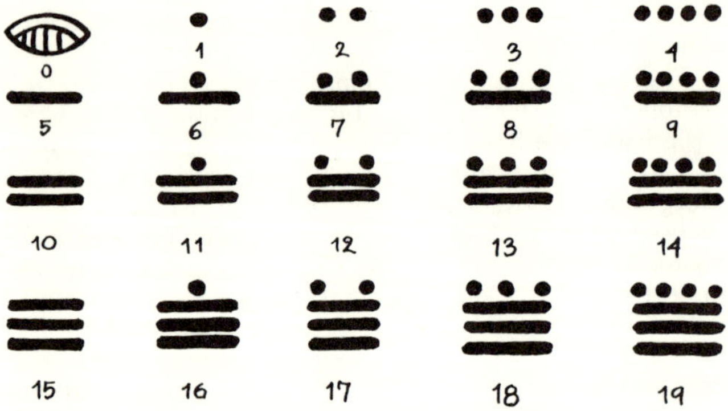

in each of the five positions, they would be registering the quantity of 168,421 in an extremely simple way, since they used only dots. To do the same we would have to use five different ideograms (1, 6, 8, 4, 2).

As examples, let us take the numbers 1975 and 8001. To write 1975, four dots would be placed in the third position (four four-hundreds or 1,600); three bars and three dots in the second (18 twenties or 360); and three bars in the first (15 units), a total of 1975. In the case of 8001, it was done by placing a dot in the fourth position (one eight-thousand); a zero in the second and third positions (zero four-hundreds and zero twenties), and a dot in the first (1 unit).

COUNTING OF TIME

The moment arrived when the Maya decided to incorporate their chronological count into their mathematical system. It is to be supposed that, among the positions mentioned, they looked for the quantity closest

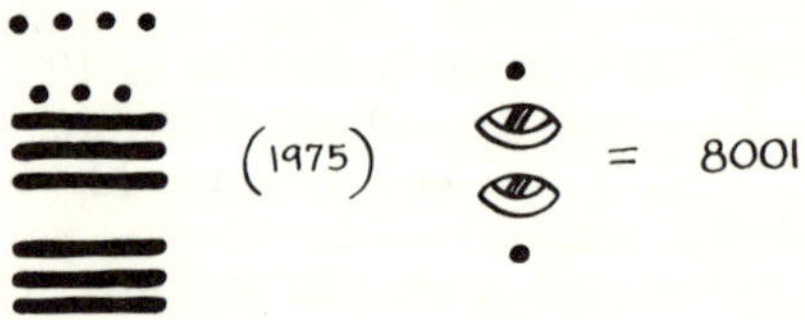

to the 365 days of their solar calendar. It is, of course, the third, that of 400. Nevertheless, if in that position they registered their years, the error to be corrected would have been very great, 35 days. They decided then to use a trick—in passing from the second to the third position, instead of multiplying 20×20, they multiplied 20×18 (the 20 days of the month by the 18 months), leaving out the 5 days uayeb. Thus they had an error of only 5 days. In the succeeding positions, multiplication was again by 20, so that in multiplying 20×360 they arrived at 7,200 instead of 8,000, and multiplying 7,200×20, the result was 144,000 instead of 160,000.

Now, referring back to the mathematical table given earlier, let us convert it to chronological counting, and speak in days rather than numbers. The lowest position is that of *kin* (sun or day) or days. The next is the *uinal* or 20 days, cited previously as a month; the following is *tun,* years of 360 days or closest to the 365 days of the Haab; the next above that of 20 tuns, called *katun,* and the uppermost one, that of 400 tuns or *baktun,* in this Initial Series system.

baktun	144,000 days	(or 20 katuns)
katun	7,200 days	(or 20 tuns)
tun	360 days	(or 18 uinals)
uinal	20 days	(or 20 kins)
kin	1 day	

For the convenience of our western mentality, when expressing a Maya date, the bars and dots are converted to Arabic numerals, and the positioning changed from vertical to horizontal, thus: 9.15.10.0.0 translates 9 baktuns, 15 katuns, 10 tuns, 0 uinals, and 0 kins counted from a predetermined date, and represents in our calendar 741 A.D.

In reality, the positions shown above were sufficient to record all of Maya history, but the Maya, in their anguished pursuit of time, were not satisfied with those positions, and calculated the tuns or years by much longer periods. The *pictun* was 8,000 tuns; the *calabtun,* 160,000 tuns; the *kinchiltun* equivalent to 3,200,000 tuns, and the *alautun,* to 64,000,000 tuns.

As an example of this type of dating, we have Stela 10 of Tikal. It bears on its face a single column of glyphs that probably announces an Initial Series composed of 1 kinchiltun (the seventh glyph, at the top of the column), 11 calabtuns, 19 pictuns, 9 baktuns, 3 katuns and 2 uinals (the glyph corresponding to kin has been weathered away). This hieroglyphic text then registers the impressive quantity of 1,841,641,600 days. And even longer periods were recorded.

It is interesting to note that most of the Maya Classic period transpired during Baktun 9 which, translated in terms of our calendar, lasted from December 9, 435 A.D. to March 13, 830 A.D.

The Maya later synthesized the recording of time, limiting themselves to what is called *u kahlay katunob* or "counting of the katuns," periods of 20 years in which a single hieroglyph could express a katun (that of the terminal day of the 20-year period, according to the Tzolkin). The date of the last day of each katun was always that of a symbol Ahau (also the sign of the sun god) preceded by a number. For that reason colonial texts, when citing only a day date (i.e. 13 Ahau), were referring to the terminal day of a particular katun.

THE STARTING DATE

Dates were recorded starting from a predetermined date which fell in the most ancient baktun, a mythical baktun since archaeology tells us that true Maya history had not yet begun. It was a day 4 Ahau 8 Cumku that, in accordance with the most accepted correlation (Goodman-Martínez-Thompson), fell in the year 3113 B.C. This does not mean, of course, that the Maya invented their calendar system at that time, and the hypothetical date is still a subject of controversy.

What did the Maya wish to record with that date? We do not know. Perhaps it was that of the creation of the first Maya who, as related in the Popol Vuh, the gods made of yellow and white corn . . .

"From *Paxil,* from *Cayalá,* so they were called, came the yellow and white ears. These are the names of the animals who brought the food: *Yac* (wildcat), *Utiú* (coyote), *Quel* (a kind of magpie) and *Hoh* (crow) . . . And thus they found the food and this was what entered into the flesh of man created, of the man formed; this was his blood, from this was made the blood of man. So entered corn (into the formation of man) thanks to the Forefathers."

RECORDING OF DATES

When the Maya wished to record a date *(see illustration following page)* on a stela, they first carved a glyph that we know as Introductory Glyph, one of whose parts was variable for it represented the profile or symbol of one of the nine gods who governed dates. It was followed by the glyphs and numerals recording the number of elapsed cycles from 4 Ahau 8 Cumku to the date carved; that is, how many baktuns, katuns, tuns, uinals and kins had passed. Then the Tzolkin date was recorded. Following there usually appeared another series of glyphs called Supplementary whose content varied and was partly hypothetical. It might be composed entirely by elements of a Lunar Series of two to seven glyphs that indicated the date in relation to the corresponding lunation (29 or 30 days) and its position within groups of lunations. At the end, the date of the solar year calendar, or Haab, generally appeared.

The Initial and Supplementary Series might be followed by a Secondary Series composed of one or more period glyphs. These glyphs indicated the time that had passed between certain pairs of dates and could serve to connect a previous or later date with that preceding it in the text; for example, that of the Initial Series. It has been suggested, among many possibilities, that the purpose of the Secondary Series was to correct the

One face of Stela E, Quiriguá, with Introductory Glyph and Initial and Supplementary Series. The date is 9.17.0.0.0. 13 Ahau 8 Cumku, approximately 771 A.D., according to Sylvanus Morley. The tallest Maya stela known, it measures 35 feet in height and weighs some 65 tons.

difference existing between the 360 days of the tun and the true duration of the solar year. But up to now, this is only theory.

The Maya also created 20 ideograms for the numbers 0 to 19, called head variants (see illustration), that frequently took the place of bars and dots. For that reason, the latter do not always appear on stelae.

To end this chapter that is simply an introduction to the Maya concept and counting of time, I quote an excerpt from the Chilam Balam of Chumayel:

> Thus was born the month,
> and it happened that the earth awakened,
> the heavens and the earth were explained,
> and the trees and rocks...
> The reading of the count of the days,
> one before the other,
> begins in the east...

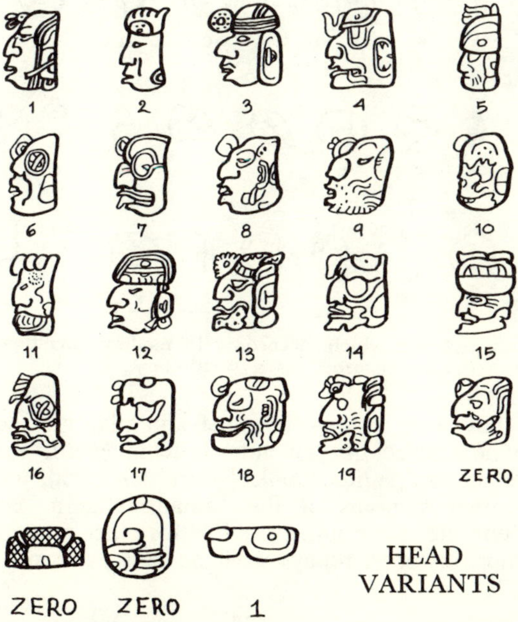

HEAD VARIANTS

MAYA LITERATURE AND THEATER

In addition to their chronological-mathematical symbols, the Maya developed a system of "literary" writing. Such texts usually accompanied the calendaric notations.

We find this type of text on stelae, stairways, mural painting, etc., as well as in the only four Maya codices that have survived to our day. Because three were sent to Europe as American curiosities, they were saved from destruction, the fate of so many volumes after the Conquest.

Landa left us some data on Maya writing in his *Relación,* without which the deciphering of those codices could perhaps never have been attempted. At the same

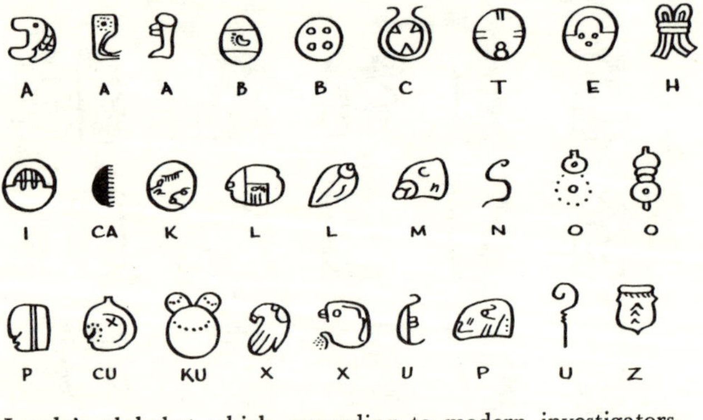

Landa's alphabet which, according to modern investigators, might better be regarded as a vocabulary.

time, however, he was the chief annihilator of codices when he carried out an auto-de-fé in Maní, Yucatán where many "painted books" were destroyed, together with other symbols of the Indian religion. But, as Brasseur de Bourbourg said, "for the modern researcher, his book repays what he destroyed in Maní."

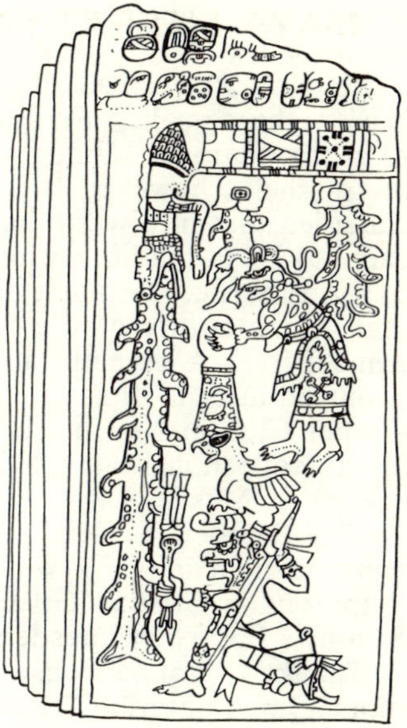

A page from the Dresden Codex. Note the way the leaves were folded to give them book form. On this page, most notable is the celestial serpent pouring water onto the earth. It appears that of the four Maya codices, the Dresden is the oldest, probably dating from around 1200 A.D.

Abbé Charles Brasseur de Bourbourg discovered numerous manuscripts concerning Maya culture. In the first place, he found the extraordinary work of Landa in the archives of the Royal Academy of Madrid. To him is due the preservation of the only Maya theatrical piece of undoubted pre-Hispanic origin, *Rabinal Achi,* and a historical text of great importance, the *Memorial de Sololá.*

And lastly, in Madrid he visited the library of Juan de Tro y Ortelano, where he found a manuscript that he called the Codex Troano, half of one of the four existing Maya codices. The second part was acquired around 1867 by a collector, José Ignacio Miró, from a certain Juan Palacios, who said it was a another Maya codex. The truth is, as shown by the French researcher León de Rosny, it was actually the second part of the

Troano and, united, they took the name of Tro-Corte-siano Codex.

Leon de Rosny had rescued another of the codices earlier, the so-called *Peresiano* or *de Paris*. He found it in the National Library of Paris. He did not find it on a shelf, however, well cared for and properly classified, but in a waste basket. No one knows how it came to be in the library or who thought its place was in the rubbish. The name Peresiano is due to the fact that in one corner of the document is written the surname Pérez. A recently authenticated codex fragment is named after its first place of exhibition in 1971, the Grolier Club in New York. The Grolier Codex is now in the collection of the National Museum of Anthropology in Mexico City.

The Dresden Codex, most important of the four, came to light in 1739 when an unknown person sold it to Johann Cristián Goetze, director of the King of Saxony's library in Dresden.

Thanks to Landa's observations and to the curiosity of a German librarian, Ernst Forstemann (1822-1906), who began studying the Maya codices as a pastime, a start was made toward deciphering Maya hieroglyphs. It was Forstemann who identified the Venus cycles of 584 days, and the value of the numerical signs according to the position they occupy on five levels, as well as the use of zero to indicate the levels that were not being utilized.

MAYA HIEROGLYPHS

Maya hieroglyphic writing is a mixed system using a combination of ideographs and phoneticism. Some signs represent entire words while others only the sound of a syllable. Currently some inscriptions can be read completely while others still elude decipherment.

Many dates could be read in the 19th century and the correlation with the Christian calendar was worked out in 1905 by J. T. Goodman. A major breakthrough came in 1958 when Heinrich Berlin argued for the presence of name glyphs on the sarcophagus lid at Palenque. He also suggested that glyphs that occurred only at one site might be the names of the sites or those of the dominant lineage.

In 1960 Tatiana Proskouriakoff published her observations on the arrangement of stelae in the front of buildings at Piedras Negras and other sites. The dates recorded on the stelae, she noted, fell within the life span of a human. One glyph, dubbed the upended frog, was always associated with the earliest date in the sequence of stelae and another, the toothache glyph, always followed the first in time. The upended frog glyph, Proskouriakoff suggested, referred to the birth

Event and Name Glyphs, according to Proskouriakoff

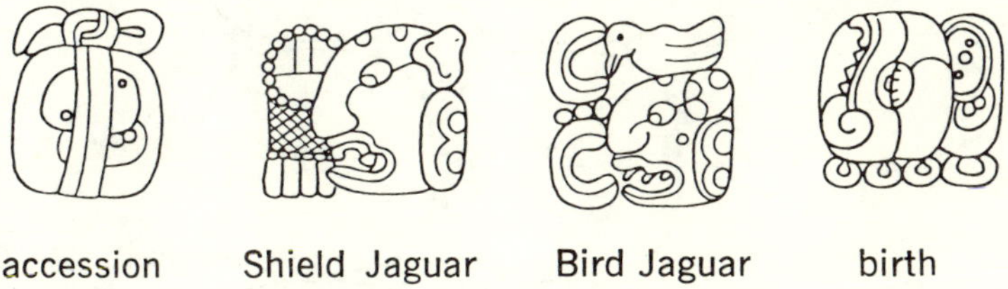

and the toothache glyph to the accession of actual rulers, not gods and priests as had been argued by others. With the decipherment of the names of Shield Jaguar and Bird Jaguar of Yaxchilán, these two Maya kings became among the first historical figures to emerge from the riddle of the carved stone monuments.

Sentence structure in Maya writing differs in the surviving codices and on ceramics and stone monuments. The typical word order on stone monuments is glyphs which express: a date or when an event took place; the verb or what action happened; the object, and the subject with name and titles. Because this preference for sentence structure was known, the word order pattern was used to identify unknown glyphs at least as to part of speech. The visual content was also an effective aid in decipherment as the picture is usually an illustration of the text.

Reading order for glyphs is typically left to right, from top to bottom across double columns of glyph blocks. Thus, the order would be A1, B1, A2, B2, A3, B3.

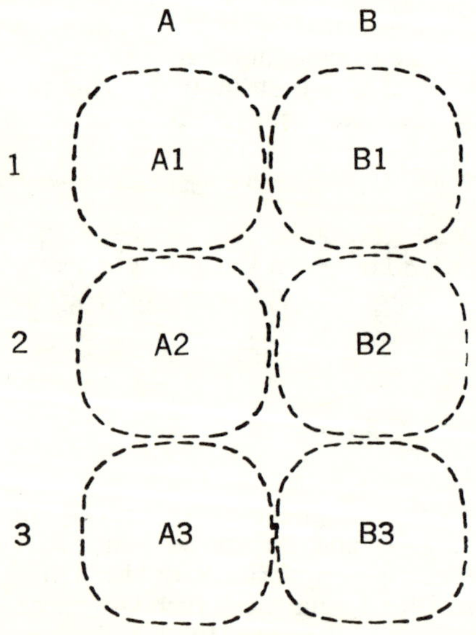

Each glyph block will have a larger main sign. Other elements, called affixes, can appear above, below, and to the left and right of the main sign. These modify the larger sign in different ways. Each block may be a word or a word may extend over to another glyph block.

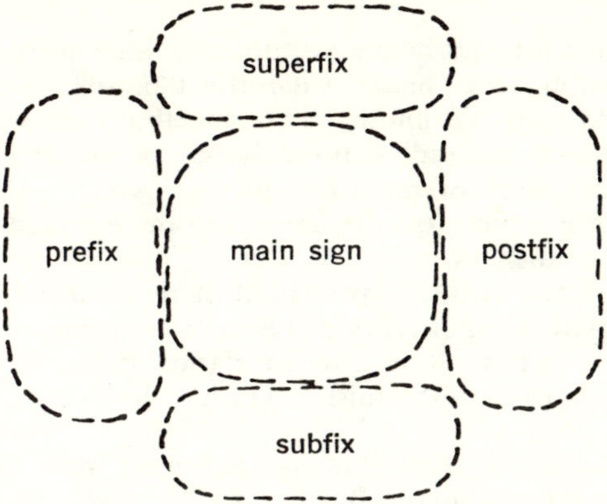

The suggestion that a phonetic component, combined with signs that stood for entire words, was part of Maya writing, was reintroduced in the 1950's by the Russian Yuri Knorosov. We now know that antecedents of modern Maya Yucatec and Chol both contributed to the phonetic signs of the hieroglyphic writing system.

WRITINGS

We know, too, that the Maya memorized their traditions and religious beliefs and transmitted them from generation to generation. Landa says: "These people also used certain characters or letters with which they wrote in their books about their ancient things and their sciences, and with these figures and some indications about them, understood their things, made others understand, and taught them."

Like the Mexicans of the central highlands, after the Conquest, Maya wise men who guarded the traditions and wisdom of their ancient culture set about recording those things in their language, using Latin characters.

There has been much discussion as to whether at least some of those colonial texts were faithful transcriptions of hieroglyphic texts, or if they were merely based on ancient chants and records passed down from father to son. We know, of course, that many prayers, moral precepts, riddles, metaphors, poems, etc., clearly of pre-Hispanic origin, are still preserved by the most conservative groups, although more or less modified by outside influences.

Some texts will be presented here to acquaint the reader with their literary richness, attempting to retain, insofar as is possible in any translation (note: two here, Maya-Spanish and Spanish-English), the original meaning in Maya.

I have chosen the following: two texts from Yucatán, one from the Chilam Balam of Chumayel that refers to the tests, in esoteric language, that had to be passed by those aspiring to the priesthood; the other, an excerpted version of the history of the Xiú and of the Itzá, as the Maya themselves set it down in the Chilam Balam of Maní—important because it shows us their concept of history and how they recorded events. From Guatemala I have selected *A Story of Witchcraft,* collected by Berendt in El Petén in 1966; and from Chiapas, a touching Tzeltal lament, collected by Jorge Díaz Olivares in Bachajón in 1969—a mother's farewell at the burial of her small son.

The Language of Zuyua and Its Meaning

"For our lord Captain Mariscal residing in Tzucuaxim at the east of Ichcaansihó, Face-of-the-birth-of-the-heavens. There he has his land, there he has his field and his manor where he lives until the day shall arrive when his work is done. Also set down is how power is bestowed by the Halach Uinics, Chiefs of great authority, and also of magnificent raiment.

"Today, fourth day of the month of September of the year 1628, we have composed what is here written in the Maya language so that whosoever may see this document may understand what is the word of Zuyua, that used by the Batabs, They-of-the-axe-of-the-towns, with the men who are the mayors (sic) and councilmen (sic).

"This was the language requested by the Halach Uinics, Chiefs of the towns, upon reaching the end of the power of 3 Ahau Katun, when the other is established, 1 Ahau Katun. This was what was in the other katun, so they said . . .

"These are the conundrums and riddles possessed by the katun that ends today, and today is the moment when the Batabs, Those-of-the-axe-of-the-towns, will be interrogated with riddles, to see if they know what it is to merit the Rule, if they know it by generation, if it is true that it is known and understood by the Batabs, Those-of-the-axe, and the Halach Uinics, Chiefs, like the chiefs they are. To see if it is true that they are descendants, the Batabs, Those-of-the-axe, of Ahaus, Princely Lords, of Halach Uinics, Chiefs. They must demonstrate it.

"This is the first riddle presented to them: Food will be requested of them. 'Bring me the Sun,' the Halach Uinic, Chief, will say to the Batabs, Those-of-the-axe. 'Bring me the Sun, my sons, to have it here in my plate. It must have the lance of the high cross thrust into the center of its heart where Yax Bolon, Green Jaguar, is placed, drinking blood. This is the speech of the Zuyua.' And this is what he requested of them: the Sun is a huge fried egg, and the lance of the high cross thrust into its heart is the blessing, and the green jaguar seated above drinking blood is the green chile when it begins to turn red. So is the speech of Zuyua.

"The second riddle presented to them is that they should go in search of the brains of heaven so that the Halach Uinic, Chief, may see them and know what size they are. 'I wish to see them, I must look at them,' he says. The brains of heaven are copal. Such is the speech of Zuyua.

"The third riddle is that they are asked to construct a large house seven *horcones* high and of a single column. This great house is the *Yahau P'ooc,* magnificent princely headdress. They will also be told to mount *Yahau Sasac Tzimin,* the horse (tapir) of princely white vestments, with a mantle, and that in their hand they carry a white rattle making it sound for Tzimin, the horse, and that the rattle shall have coagulated blood. A speech that comes from Zuyua. The white horse requested is the sandal of henequen fiber and the white mantle and white rattle are the *Flores de Mayo* (frangipangi), and the coagulated blood is the golden yellow of the flower and symbolizes that the Flor de Mayo comes from the blood of offerings, the blood of those bereft of father and mother, from the miserable ones. So is the speech of Zuyua.

"The fourth riddle is that they shall go to their homes, saying to them: 'My children, when you return to see me, it shall be precisely when the Sun is in the middle of the heavens, you shall be two and you shall come very close together, my youths, and when you arrive here your dog shall come behind you and shall carry in his teeth the soul of Cilich Colel, Sacred Lady, when you shall come. The speech of Zuyua.' The two youths referred to as coming together just at midday are he himself when he comes stepping on his shadow, and the dog he asked to come with them is his own wife, and the soul of Cilich Colel, Sacred Lady, represents the great candles (sic), axes (sic) of wax. Thus is the speech of Zuyua.

"The fifth riddle is to request that they search for the heart of *Ku Citbil ti Caan,* Lord-deity-of-the-heavens, and when they bring it, that it shall be borne on thirteen flat layers, and that it shall come swathed in rough white vestments. The heart of Ku Citbil, Lord-deity, requested of them is the stone *Kan,* Corn, the precious stone, and its bed of thirteen flat layers is *Yahau Uah,* Pudding-of-corn-tortillas-of-thirteen-layers-filled-with-beans, and the rough white cloth in which it comes wrapped is the white napkin. Thus is the speech of Zuyua."

Excerpts from the History of the Xiú and of the Itzá in the Land of the Maya

In said Katun
they left their land and their home:
Nonoualcan.
There were the Tutul Xiú,
to the west of Zuiná.
The land from whence they came:
Tulapa Chicunauhtlan . .

Ah Mekat Tutul Xiú
arrived in Chacnouitan.
One year less
than one hundred years
they were there, in Chacnouitan.
Then was discovered
the region of Ziyan-Caan
there, in Bakhalal . . .

The years of their rule in Bakhalal
ended.

Thus, then,
they appeared here,
in Chichén Itzá.
Eleven Ahau, nine Ahau, seven Ahau,
five Ahau, three Ahau, one Ahau.
One hundred and twenty years they ruled
Chichén Itzá.

Then Chichén Itzá was abandoned.
They went to settle Chanputun.
There were the houses
of the Itzá,
men deified. There.

Six Ahau.
The land of Chanputun was seized. . .

They abandoned Chanputun. . .

They were the Itzá
under the tree, under the ashes,
under the reeds.
There they suffered. . .

Ah Cuitok Tutulxiú established himself
in Uxmal. . .

Two hundred years they ruled,
their Halach-uinicil, True Men,
in Chichén Itzá and Mayapán. . .

The Halach-uinicil, True Man,
abandoned Chichén Itzá
because of the sinful word of Hunaceel Cauich
against Chacxibchac of Chichén Itzá.

Because of the sinful speech of Hunaceel,
Halach-uinicil, True Man
of Mayapán, the Walled Place,
that occurred in the ninetieth year.
This happened in the tenth year of eight Ahau.

That Katun they abandoned it (Chichén Itzá),
Ah Tzinteyutchan and Tzuntecum
and Taxcal and Pantemit, Xuch-ueuet
and Itzcuat and Kakaltecat,
these were the names
of the great ones of Mayapán. . .

Mayapán was destroyed by a foreigner
Ah Uitzil, the Lord of the Hills,
Tancah Mayapán. . .

Katuns six Ahau, four Ahau,
two Ahau.

That year was the first step,
the arrival of the Spaniards,
who saw for the first time
our land,
the province of Yucatán,
sixty years
after the destruction of the Walled Place.

Thirteen Ahau, eleven Ahau.
Occurred the death of Maya people on the ramparts,
and great fever, smallpox. . .

In nine Ahau Christianity began,
there was baptism.
Within that Katun
arrived the first Bishop, Toral,
that was his name.

A Story of Witchcraft

A man married a woman without knowing she was a witch.
One day he said to her: "Crush two measures of salt."
She first crushed them and then asked:
"What do you want it for?"

One night the man was awake and saw his wife go out.
He took his axe and followed her secretly to the woods.
When they arrived at a small clearing,
there the moon shone brightly.
The man took shelter beneath a great Ceiba tree.
Then she took off her clothes, the woman.
She let them fall behind her and nude, facing
the moon, she shed her skin,
and stood there in just her bones.
Then she ascended to the sky.

When she descended, he asked her:
"Do you reach the sky by yourself?"
But she wasn't able to ascend again
because he sprinkled the salt on her.

Upon the Death of a Child

Little flower of my womb, image of your father,
portrait of your mother.
Why are you going so far away?
Why do you leave me in loneliness?
Why does your heart no longer beat?
Did I not give you life with great pain and suffering?
I gave you to suck at my breast, I gave you food.
I protected you from birth.
Where is your sainted soul?
Why did you go away from me?
My heart is parting in two,
my heart grows weak,
my heart is prostrate and heavy
because of your death.
Your leaving is destroying me,
my little son, my little bird.
Where are you?
Little flower of my womb,
my heart is lonely
and calls for your companionship.

This text is repeated over and over again until the mother manages to somewhat assuage her grief.

Dramatic art deserves a separate mention since there is interesting material available. Landa left us two texts transcribed and analyzed below. The first is in Chapter XXII of his work, and reads as follows:

"The Indians have very amusing entertainment and especially that of players, presented with much wit (*a*); so much so that the Spaniards hire them so they may see themselves caricatured in the mimicked conversations that pass between their maids, spouses or themselves... acted out with artifice and talent.

"They have small kettledrums that they beat with their hands, and another kettledrum of hollow wood with a heavy, sad sound (*b*) that they play with a long stick with the milk of a tree on one end (*c*); and they have long, slender trumpets, of hollowed-out sticks, and at the ends, some long, twisted gourds, and they have another instrument (that they make) of the whole turtle with its shell, and once the flesh is removed they play it with the palm of the hand and its sound is lugubrious and sad.

"They have whistles made from the hollowed-out long bones of deer (*d*), and great conch shells (*e*) and reed flutes (*f*), and with these instruments accompany the brave ones. Especially there are two dances very much worth seeing (*g*). One is a game with reeds and so they call it *colomché* (*h*), which is what it means. To play it, a large circle of dancers gather, with their musical accompaniment, and to its beat two dancers separate from the circle, one with a handful of reed darts, dancing in an upright position, the other dancing in a crouch, and both in time with those of the circle. The one with the darts throws them at the other with all his strength, and the latter, with great skill, knocks them away with a small bat. When they have finished, they return to the ring, without losing the beat, and two others come out to do the same.

"There is another dance (*i*) in which some 800 Indians, more or less, take part, divided into small bands, with martial music and step, and not one loses step, and their dances are

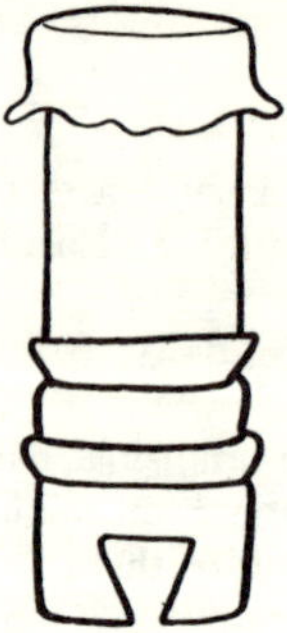

PAX

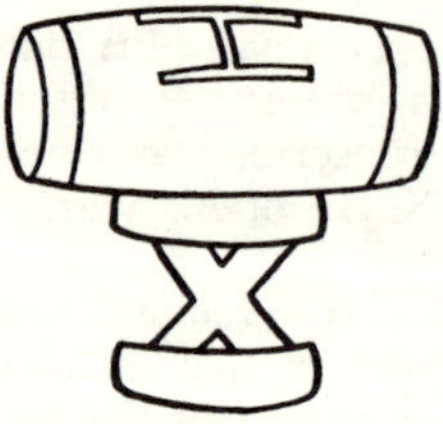

TUNKUL

tiring because they dance all day, and food and drink are taken to them. It was not the custom of the men to dance with the women."

This account by Landa tells us clearly of the existence of theatrical representations among the Maya. The statement signalled (*a*) is confirmed by a parallel text from an interesting book published in 1601, entitled *Historia General de los Hechos de los Castellanos en las Islas y Tierra Firme del Mar Océano,* by Antonio de Herrera y Tordesillas: "It was their custom to have actors at their fiestas and they wore costumes, and it was their custom to imitate the gestures of the Spaniards around them, and their performances were so well executed and elegantly done that they caused laughter."

Herrera also gives complementary data on the musical instruments mentioned by Landa in (*b*). He says the Maya "used small drums, and drums hollowed out of a piece of wood that had a hoarse sound (used also in other regions of the Indies)."

He then listed additional musical instruments: the *tunkul* was a horizontal drum; the *pax,* a vertical drum, although the term "pax" appears to have been used in later times as a verb: "to play some instrument with the hands." Among present-day Lacandón a similar drum is used and held to be the god of song, *Kayum.* The vertical drum is represented in the Dresden and Tro-Cortesian codices, as well as in the mural paintings of Bonampak.

Cogolludo also refers to musical instruments: "When they were idol worshipers and even now, they dance and sing like the Mexicans. They have a chief singer who gives the pitch and teaches what is necessary to be able to sing. They venerate and respect this man, and he is given a special place at the fiestas and in meetings. They call him *Holpop,* and he is entrusted with the drums or tunkuls, as well as other musical instruments, like trumpets, conch shells and other things they use. The tunkul is made of hollowed-out wood and some are so large that their sound is heard for two leagues when the wind comes from that direction. They chant their fables and ancient traditions."

Concerning (*c*), the "milk of a tree" refers to rubber. The Maya called it *kik,* meaning blood. Landa also speaks of balls of kik used as incense.

As for (*d*), the only representation of these instruments in the codices is found in the Dresden, where a black figure appears, playing a flute-like instrument that seems to be of bone. Insofar as (*e*) is concerned, the Lacandón still use a conch trumpet to call upon the gods to descend and share in the offerings. The Lacandón also have large reed flutes like that mentioned in (*f*). Landa makes no reference to rattles, although they are frequently represented in the codices and have been found in archaeological explorations, like that of the Sacred Well of Chichén Itzá. They are employed in Lacandón and Yucatec Maya religious ceremonies.

Very little is known about pre-Hispanic Maya dances other than the information given by Landa in (*g*). We know that the men generally danced alone, and that the old women had their own dance. There was also an erotic dance performed by men and women. In the *Relación de Campocolché,* after a description of walking on fire (still performed by the Tzotzil during Carnival), it is stated: "There were many other dances, at least 1,000 different ones, and they gathered to see them, and they considered them of great importance, and as many as 15,000 Indians gathered, from as far as 30 leagues distant, to see them because. . . they regarded them as something very important."

Colomché (*h*) is a term worth trying to elucidate. Of the various meanings given in the *Diccionario de Motul* for the root *col,* the most appropriate to interpret our term is *col-ak,* "withdraw something." *Om* is an old Maya suffix meaning "he who does." Thus, from *cay* (fish) is formed *cayom,* fisherman; from *pat* (clay pot), *patom,* potter, etc. And finally, *ché* means sliver, wood, tree. Therefore, we can translate colomché as "he who withdraws a rod, a sliver."

Following (*i*), Landa describes an impressive dance called *Holcan okot* or *Batel okot,* a warrior dance performed in the years called *muluc* and in the month *Pax.* It appears that during the dance a young man was sacrificed, and that a dramatic chant accompanied the action. The text was perhaps the one preserved in the manuscript called *The Songs of Dzitbalché*:

Spy, stalker who hunts in the hills,
once, twice,
let us go to the hunt along the edge of the grove
in rapid rhythm, even three times.
Lift up your head.
Sharpen well your eyes.
Make no errors,
so you will not miss your prize.
Is the point of your dart well sharpened?
Is your bow well strung?
Have you put good *catzim* resin on the feathers
that adorn the shaft of your dart?
Have you rubbed deer grease on the muscles of your arm,
your foot, your knees, your calves,
your ribs, your chest, your breast?
Make three fast turns
around the column of painted stone,
over there where the virile young man,
chaste and immaculate, is bound.
Make the first, and on the second turn

lift up your bow, fit the arrow to the string,
aim at his breast. It is not necessary
to use all your force
when you let fly, so that his flesh
will not be too deeply wounded,
so that he may suffer a little
as the Lord God wished.
When you make the second turn
around the column painted blue,
as you do it,
shoot another arrow at him.
You must do this,
never ceasing to dance, because
that is how the great, noble warriors do it,
the men who are chosen
to please in the eyes of the Lord God.
Just as the sun sends out its first rays
over the woods to the east,
the archer-bowman begins his chant.
They give their all,
the shield-bearing warriors.

Continuing with Landa's texts, there is another very informative one on theatrical representations. Referring to the festivities held in the month of Xul, he says:

"On 16 Xul (Landa clearly made an error here since the days were counted from 1 to 13), all the lords and priests gathered in Maní, and with them came great multitudes from the villages, already prepared through fasting and abstinence. That day, in the afternoon, there was a great procession of people, and with many of their play actors, from the lord's house where they had gathered, who went serenely to the Temple of Kukulkán which had been greatly adorned... Until the first day of Yaxkin (the following month) the actors wandered about those five days giving performances in the principal houses, and collecting the gifts made to them, and they carried them all off to the temple where, at the end of the five days, they divided the gifts among the lords, priests and dancers, and took the banners and the idols and returned to the lord's house from whence each returned to his own. . ."

Although Landa was acquainted with Chichén Itzá, he mentions only a few of the buildings in that immense city. He says:

"In front was the North Stairway (now called the Castle, or Temple of Kukulkán) and at a short distance, two small theaters of stone, with four stairways, paved on top, where it is said that they performed the farces and comedies for the pleasure of the people. From the patio in front of these theaters, a beautiful broad highway leads to a well about two stone-throws away."

The Castle, the Temple at the Sacred Well, and these two small theaters, are the only structures Landa mentions in Chichén. Today, the "theaters" are known as the Platform of Venus and the Platform of the Eagles. Perhaps these temples were the setting for a performance mentioned by Antonio de Ciudad Real in the *Relación de Ponce*: ". . . some masked men that, dancing and with graceful gestures, also imitated very naturally the song of certain night birds of that land. There was flute and trumpet music."

To conclude this chapter let us examine a passage from the only Maya play of pre-Hispanic origin that has come down to us in almost complete form—*Rabinal Achi* or "The Varón of Rabinal" (Varón: Man of Respectability). The play continued to be presented for three centuries after the Conquest, until about 1820. Thirty years later, in 1850, the last person who knew the play via oral tradition, Bartolo Zis—an inhabitant of the village where it was enacted, San Pedro de Rabinal, Guatemala—set it down in writing as a legacy to his descendants. Abbé Charles Brasseur de Bourbourg translated it in 1862.

The plot is very simple. The Varón of Rabinal, son of Chief Five-Rain, defeats the Varón of the Queché in battle and, after making him his prisoner, takes him before his father. The latter grants the conquered one various last favors, and afterwards, as was the fate of all warrior prisoners, the Varón of the Queché is sacrificed. Performance of the play is accompanied by dancing and music.

Chief Five-Rain

Brave one, varón, man of the Cavek-Queché: thanks to the heavens, thanks to the earth, you have arrived within the vast walls, in the vast fortress where I extend my hands, extend my shadow, I the grandfather, Chief Five-Rain.

Therefore, say, reveal, why did you imitate the howl of the coyote, the cry of the fox, the sound of the weasel, beyond the vast walls, beyond the vast fortress, to tempt, to attract my innocent children, my innocent sons; to draw them away from the vast walls, the vast fortress, in Iximché; to search out, to find the golden honey, the new honey of the bees, the food that was for me, the grandfather, Chief Five-Rain, within the vast walls, within the vast fortress.

It was you who seized the nine, the ten innocent children, innocent sons who were about to be carried off to the Queché mountains, to the Queché valleys, if my fearlessness, my bravery had not been alert; because there you would have cut the root, the trunk of the innocent children, innocent sons.

You came also to seize me, there in The Baths. There I was captured by the child of your arrow, the child of your shield.

You confined me in the stone, limestone, in the Queché mountains, in the Queché valleys; there you would have cut my root, my trunk, in the Queché mountains, the Queché valleys.

That was why my brave one, my varón, the greatest of all, the Varón of Rabinal, freed me from there, tore me away from there, with the aid of the child of his arrow, the child of his shield.

If my brave one, my varón, had not existed, truly you would have cut my root, my trunk.

So they brought me again to the vast walls, the vast fortress. You also razed two, three towns. . .

When will the desire of your heart, your willfulness, your daring no longer dominate you? How long will you allow them to move you, allow them to excite you?

That stubbornness, that daring, were they not buried, hidden, in Coton, in Tikiram, in Beleheh Nokoh, in Beleheh Chumay?

Did not we the governors, we the commanders have that willfulness, that daring buried, hidden in each of the walls of the fortress?

But you shall pay for that here, under the heavens, upon the earth. You have said, then, goodbye to your mountains, to your valleys, because here you shall die, you shall perish, under the heavens, upon the earth.

May the heavens, the earth, be with you, man of the Cavek-Queché!

The Varón of the Queché

Chief Five-Rain, give me your approval before the heavens, before the earth. In truth here are the words, in truth here are the opinions you have expressed before the heavens, before the earth; in truth I have done wrong.

Your voice also said: "Have you not tempted, called to the innocent children, the innocent sons, to lure them to hunt for, to discover the golden honey, the new honey of the bees, the food destined for me, the grandfather, Chief Five-Rain, within the vast walls, within the vast fortress?"

So spoke your voice. In truth I did wrong, driven by the desire in my heart, because I had not been able to possess myself of those lovely mountains, of those lovely valleys, here under the heavens, upon the earth.

Your voice also said: "It was you who came to seize me; who overpowered me in The Baths." Thus spoke your voice. In truth I have done wrong, driven by the desire of my heart.

Your voice also said: "You razed two, three towns. . ." So was your word.

In truth, I did wrong, driven by the desire of my heart, because I had not been able to possess myself of those lovely mountains, lovely valleys, here under the heavens, upon the earth.

Your voice also said: "Say goodbye to your mountains, to your valleys; raise your voice, because here you shall die, you shall perish; here we shall cut your root, your trunk; here under the heavens, upon the earth." That was what your voice said.

In truth, I disobeyed your voice, your commandments, here before the heavens, before the earth, driven by the desire of my heart.

If I must die here, perish here, then this is what my voice says to your lips, to your face: Now that you are well supplied, well provisioned within the high walls, in the high fortress, grant me your food, your drink: those princely drinks called Ixtatzunun: the twelve beverages, the twelve liquids, intoxicating, sweet, refreshing, gay, attrahent, that are to be drunk before sleep, in the vast walls, in the vast fortress...

I shall taste them fleetingly, as the supreme sign of my death, of my demise, under the heavens, upon the earth. That is my word.

May the heavens, the earth be with you, Chief Five-Rain!

Chief Five-Rain

Brave one, Varón, Man of the Cavek-Queché. Your voice proclaimed to the heavens, to the earth: "Grant me your food, your drink. I shall receive them to try them." So spoke your voice. Well, I shall give them to you; I shall grant them to you. Servants, bring forth my food, my drink. Let them be given to that brave one, that Varón, that man of the Cavek-Queché, as the supreme sign of his death, of his demise, here below the heavens, upon the earth.

A Servant

As you wish, my lord, my ruler. I shall give them to that brave one, to that Varón, man of the Cavek-Queché.

The servants bring in a table loaded with delicacies of food and drink.

Taste some of the food, of the drink of my lord, my ruler, the grandfather, Chief Five-Rain, within the vast confines, in the vast fortress, in the retreat of my lord, my ruler, valiant Varón.

The Varón of the Queché

He eats and drinks, disdainfully. Then he dances before the court. He then returns and says:

Oh, Chief Five-Rain, is that your food, is that your drink? In truth there is nothing to say, nothing to be found in either to recommend them to my lips, to my person. If only you could sample for an instant, in my mountains, in my valleys, the attrahent, pleasing, gay, sweet, refreshing liquids that I imbibe in my mountains, in my valleys!

My voice speaks thus to the heavens, to the earth:

Is that the table of your delicacies; is that the cup from which you drink? But that is the skull of my grandfather; that is the head of my father, that which I see, that which I contemplate. Could not the same be done with the bones of my head, with the bones of my skull; chisel out my mouth, sculpture my face?

In this way, upon leaving my mountains, my valleys, my children, my sons will say: "Here is the skull of our grandfather, of our father."

So shall speak my children, my sons, here, from dawn to dusk. . .

PROPHECIES OF THE CONQUEST

Documents written *after* the Conquest by Indians and Europeans contain certain obscure passages that have been interpreted as Prophecies or Predictions. Although we cannot be positive, it is entirely likely that the Indian writings resulted from a mixture of traditional texts preserved orally for centuries, with western-Christian interpolations.

The European chroniclers, who had access to these texts shortly after the Conquest, hastened to interpret them as prophecies heralding the Conquest. This served to bolster their theological fervor, since otherwise, if the Indians had not in some way received revelation or illumination from the only true God, it could not be explained how the natives, with only "natural light," had created such extraordinary cultures and philosophies. And, in a series of Maya cruciform symbols, the Spaniards sought to identify the Cross of Christ that, too, must have been given to the Indians through divine revelation.

No one has yet attempted an analysis of the dialectics used by the European chroniclers to prove the foregoing, but it would be very interesting in that it would tell us much of their way of thinking (the majority were friars and priests) as well as explain to modern ethnohistorians the why of many approaches and solutions to problems that resulted from the cultural clash.

Among the known books of Chilam Balam, that of Maní was copied by Juan Pío Pérez directly from Maya manuscripts written by Indians after the Conquest. One of the texts was interpreted by chronicler Diego López de Cogolludo as a prophecy announcing the Conquest and the arrival of the True God. Juan Pío Pérez copied the Maya texts in the 19th century, and Cogolludo wrote his history in the 17th century. Two hundred years apart, but both had access to the same material.

Diego de Landa, Yucatán's first chronicler, was also acquainted with it. Now, let us take up the three versions.

I translate the original Maya text of Pío Pérez as follows:

When the root of 13 Ahau Katun comes to an end
it shall pass that the Itzá will see,
it shall pass that they will see there in Tancah
the sign of the Lord, the Only God.
He will arrive. The sacred wood will be displayed,
set above the peoples, so that the earth
may be illuminated.
Lord: consolation is no more.
Envy is no more
because on this day the bearer of the sign will have arrived.
Oh Lord, thy word will come to submerge itself in the
peoples of the earth!
From the north, from the east shall come the master,
oh powerful Itzamná!
Thy master is coming to thy people, oh Itzá!
He is coming to enlighten thy people.
Receive thy guests, the bearded ones,
the bearers of the sign of God.
Lord, good is the word of the God who comes to us,
he who comes to thy people with words about
the day of resurrection.
Because of that there will be no fear on earth.
Lord, thou, the Only God, he who created us,
is the sign of the divine word valid?
Lord: the new wood is substituted for the old...

Landa probably had direct access to the text. He wrote his history in 1566, and the original is undoubtedly earlier. He has the following to say about the prophecy of the Chilam Balam of Maní:

"In the same way that the Mexican nation had signs and prophecies of the coming of the Spaniards, and of the destruction of its power and its religion, so did the population of Yucatán some years before the Adelantado Montejo conquered them; and, in the mountains of Maní, which is in the province of the Tutul Xiú, an Indian named Cambal (who held the) office (of) Chilam (which means) 'he who has the duty of giving the answers of the god (demonio)' announced to them publicly that they soon would be subjected by a foreign people, and that they would preach to them One God and the power of a tree, which in their language is called *vamanché* which means 'a tree erected with great virtue against the evil spirit.' "

Landa, therefore, considered the text equally prophetic, and the "tree" (interpreted as the cross of Christ) he calls "vamanché."

Finally, let us see what Cogolludo says. I have presented my version of the prophecy, as faithful to the original Maya as possible. I shall not analyze here the differences as compared with Cogolludo's version, which are obvious since he translated it as he deemed convenient to the end of proving that Christianity had been revealed to the Maya before the arrival of the Spaniards. Cogolludo translated it thus, adding phrases at will:

"At the end of the 13th age and at the height of their power, to Ytzá and the city of Tancah... will come the sign of God who is in Heaven, and the Cross will be revealed to the world... Men will be divided when this sign be brought in the future. Priests, before going a league, even a quarter league, you shall behold the Cross, it shall appear and it shall become as dawn to you from Pole to Pole. The cult to many gods shall end. Now our father comes, Oh Ytzalamnos. Now comes our brother, Tantunites. Receive our bearded guests from the east who come to bring the sign of God. It is God who comes to us, meek and pious. Good are the words of God. Yea, we exalt thy sign on high, we exalt it to worship and look upon it. We must exalt the Cross. In opposition to the lie, it appears today, in opposition to the first tree of the world. Today it is demonstrated to the world. This is the sign of God on high. Worship it, oh Ytzalana people, let us worship it with honest will, let us worship Him who is our God, the true God. Receive the word of the true God, since he who speaks to us comes from the heavens. Acquire wisdom and be truly those of Ytzá. Those who believe shall be enlightened in the age to come. Listen, if it matters to you what I say, I warn and charge you. I, your interpreter and accredited teacher. Balam is my name. And with this I have finished saying what the true God bade me, so that the world might hear."

CAME THE CONQUERORS

Whether these prophecies were born of foresight or hindsight is immaterial: the conquest of the Maya was, in fact, carried out between 1527 and 1546. Spanish domination was not complete, however, until 1697 when the Itzá of Tayasal ceased their resistance.

In contrast to Cortés' subjugation of the Aztecs—a united people, concentrated in their island capital of Tenochtitlan—in a period of only two years, the conquest of Maya territory, where the divided, sometimes warring groups were scattered over a vast area, was slow and spasmodic.

The events that brought to a tragic end the ancient and matchless Maya culture are painful to contemplate. A brief listing of the highlights of that long-drawn-out struggle will suffice:

1523-25 Pedro de Alvarado subdued the Maya of Guatemala.

1526 Francisco de Montejo received a royal permit to conquer the "Islands of Campeche and Yucatán," together with the title of *Adelantado,* pioneer or explorer.

1527 Montejo's party landed at Cabo Catoche and made the first unsuccessful attempt at conquest.

1531 He founded the town of Campeche and colonization began.

1534 Fray Jacobo de Testera, a Franciscan missionary, arrived in Campeche, establishing monasteries there and in Champotón. Other Franciscans followed, proving more successful than armies in consolidating the conquest.

1542 Francisco de Montejo, son of the Adelantado, founded the city of Mérida on the site of town of T'Hó.

1543 Valladolid founded on the site of Zací.

1546 Last hold-out groups in the eastern portion of the Peninsula were subdued.

1697 Island kingdom of Tayasal in Lake Petén Itzá forced to submit to Spanish rule.

The *dzules,* the foreigners, had arrived, bringing a new order, destroying the old: that of the sun, of time, of the magnificent cities.

And of the Maya, the Chilam Balam of Chumayel has this to say:

"Their spirit held no love for Dzules nor for their Christianity. Tribute was not paid to them (dzules) by the spirit of the birds, nor by that of the precious stones, nor of the sculptured stones (stelae), nor of the tigers who protected them (the Maya). Sixteen hundred years and three hundred more ended their life. They knew how to count time, even within themselves. The moon, the wind, the year, the day, they all move, but also pass on. All blood reaches its place of rest, as all power reaches its throne... Measured were the days of the beneficence of the sun, of the latticework formed by the stars from whence the gods look down upon us. The good lords of the stars, all good.

"There was health, devotion; there was no sickness, aching bones, fever or smallpox; no pains in chest or stomach. They walked with their bodies held tall. But the Dzules came and undid everything. They taught fear. They withered the flower, they sucked until they killed the flowers of others so theirs would live. They killed the flower of the Nacxit Xuchitl. No longer were there priests to teach us. And the second era was established, began to rule, and it was the cause of our death. Without priests, without wisdom, without courage, without shame, everyone the same. There was no longer great wisdom, nor word nor teaching of the lords. The gods that arrived here were worthless! The Dzules came only to castrate the Sun! And the children of their children have stayed with us, and we receive only their bitterness..."

EPILOGUE

In this book I have set down something of the little we know of the Maya. Many things are still a mystery and may always remain so. Perhaps the Maya scholar suffers the punishment that the Forefathers, the Creator and the Maker, imposed on man, a punishment that prevents him from broadening his vision.

This limitation on man is related in the Popol Vuh when, after various attempts, the gods were finally able to create man. . .

"Then the Creator and the Maker asked the four men who were created:

"What do you think of your state? Can you not see? Can you not hear? Your language and your way of walking, are they not good? Look around you then! Contemplate the world! See if the mountains and valleys do not appear! Try then to see! they said to them, and thereupon the men saw all that there was in the world. The men then thanked the Creator and the Maker. Verily, we thank ye, over and over. We have been created, we have been given a mouth and a face, we speak, hear, think and walk; we are in possession of our senses, and we are acquainted with all that is far and near. We also see the large and the small in the heavens and on earth. We thank ye, then, for having given us being, oh grandmother, oh grandfather!

"They finished learning about everything, and examined the four corners and the four points of the vault of the sky and the face of the earth.

"But the Creator and the Maker were not pleased with what they had heard... It is not right what our creatures, our handiwork say. They know everything, the large and the small, they said.

"And so the Forefathers again held council: What shall we do with them now? Let their sight encompass only that which is near, let them see only a little of the earth's face. It is not right what they say. Are they not by their nature mere creatures, puppets? Must they also be gods?

"...Let us curb a little their desires, for what we see is not good. Why should they be like us, their authors, we who can see over great distances, who know and see all?... so they spoke, and thereupon changed the nature of their creation, their creatures.

"Then the Heart of the Sky cast a vapor over their eyes, which were clouded as when one blows upon a mirror. Their eyes were misted and they could see only what was near. Only that was clear to them.

"So were destroyed the wisdom and knowledge of the four men, origin and beginning..."

SOURCES FOR STUDYING THE MAYA

Our knowledge of the ancient Maya has been supplied chiefly by the various anthropological specialties: ethno-history, ethnography, linguistics, and archaeology are our research tools.

For a very long period of Maya culture we must rely exclusively upon archaeology and its sister sciences, like paleontology. For a later period we can go to such colonial sources as the chronicles, histories, and documents composed—in Spanish and Maya—by Europeans and Indians. After the Conquest, the Indians early learned to record in Latin characters their history and achievements, previously preserved through oral tradition. Although they could not avoid Western-Christian interpolations, they did not lose sight of the value of keeping alive their cultural heritage, and therefore wrote it down.

More recently, thanks to cultural conservatism, we have had at our disposal an extremely important source made up of ethnographic and ethnohistorical studies. Ethnography is the science that describes the culture, customs, behavior, and characteristic ways of life of human groups, while ethnohistory determines the cultural and social structure of peoples at a given moment in history. The usefulness of these sciences is clear when, as in the case of the Maya, investigators are concerned with a native group that has persevered in cultivating its past through oral tradition and the continued observance of ancient ways.

All of these sources have contributed to this book. However, since they are the least known despite their undoubted value, following are some of the colonial sources, written by both Indians and Europeans. Inasmuch as space precludes the listing of all such colonial documents, I shall mention only the most important from the area where Yucatec-Maya is spoken. Let us begin with the dictionaries and vocabularies, indispensable in investigating the Maya, although they were not compiled by Indians.

16th-Century Dictionaries

The Dictionary of Villalpando was published in Mexico in 1571. It is probably based on the vocabulary contained in his *Arte*, which was lost. (*"Arte"* was the term used to designate grammars of Indian tongues.)

Antonio de Ciudad Real, a companion of Diego de Landa, was the author of various works in Maya. He arrived in America in 1573 and died in 1617. His *Gran Diccionario de Calepino* was prepared in two copies, neither of which has been found. It was said he spent 40 years in writing it, and the historian Cogulludo said of him: "He learned the Maya language of these Indians with such perfection that he was the greatest teacher of them ever known in this land. In Maya he preached, taught, and wrote Sermons of the Saints ....."

The *Dictionary of Motul* is the most famous of existing Maya dictionaries, and probably was compiled in the last quarter of the 16th century. A copy of this manuscript is in the John Carter Brown Library at Providence, Rhode Island. It is called the Dictionary of Motul because there is reason to believe that the first part was written in the Convent of Motul, Yucatán. Although it is impossible to fix the exact date of its preparation, the author speaks of a comet he saw in 1577, and makes reference to the fact that he was writing "in the first generation after the Conquest." The existing copy consists of two parts: Maya-Spanish and Spanish-Maya. The latter section, alone, contains some 11,180 words and was probably written after the Maya-Spanish part. There is good reason to belileve that the Maya-Spanish section may be the Calepino of Ciudad Real, mentioned above. The ethnographic content of the Motul Dictionary is invaluable.

Mention must be made of the Maya words listed by Gonzalo Fernández de Oviedo y Valdés in his *Historia General de las Indias*, written in 1535; and the vocabulary of Maya words in Fray Diego de Landa's work, extracted and translated by Charles P. Bowditch at the beginning of this century. The work is preserved in the Berendt collection of Philadelphia.

Vocabularies of the 18th and 19th Centuries

No more such works were published until 1746 when the vocabulary of Pedro Beltrán de Santa Rosa, an Indian Franciscan, appeared. He included many medical and biological terms, of which 150 refer to the anatomical knowledge possessed by the Maya at the time of the Conquest. This Maya-Spanish vocabulary was published again in 1898, together with a Spanish-Maya vocabulary composed by Juan Pío Pérez in Ticul around 1835.

Other Colonial Sources, 16th to 19th Centuries

The Books of *Chilam Balam*, or Priest Balam, which was the name given to a famous seer just before the Conquest. He was not the source for all of the books, it is simply a name given to them for convenience and, in addition, each bears the name of the village where it was compiled, i.e., the Chilam Balam of Chumayel, Tizimin, Ixil, Nah, Tekax, Tusik, Kaua, Maní (also known as the Pérez Codex), Peto, Nabula, Oxkutzcab, Tihosuco, Tixkahal and Hocabá. Gates speaks of another one from Teabo. Their contents can be divided into historical texts (chronicles and brief histories) and non-historical material (prophecies, mythical–religious, medical, and astrological texts).

There are several documents dedicated to the sudy of herbal medicine, like the *Libro del Judio* (Book of the Jew), the *Libro de Sotuta*, that of *Mena*, and the extraordinary *Ritual of the Bacab* (translated into English by Ralph Roys). The last-mentioned might be considered the Maya equivalent of the Papyrus of Ebers on Egyptian medicine. It is a document of the 18th century, or perhaps the 17th, from Yucatán, containing 42 texts of a magical nature, a long list of curative plants, and instructions for herb doctors. The list of herbs includes those used for treating a wide range of wounds, and illnesses, such as fright, asthma, toothache, respiratory congestion and bone diseases. There are prescriptions for treatment of gout, erysipelas, fever, ulcers, detachment of the placenta, etc. At the end of the book are ten pages of ordinary medical prescriptions, totally different from the main text in content and handwriting. Two of the pages were written on the back of an Indulgence printed in 1779. The only allusions to Spain and Christianity in the entire text are found in this last section.

There are also chronicles llike those of Calkiní, Chicxulub, and Yaxkukul; of the latter we know the name of the author, a Maya called Macau Pech.

Additional ancient manuscripts have turned up in recent years. One is *Los Cantares* or Songs of Dzitbalché (a sample of which is offered on page 118), found in Mérida in 1942 but bearing the name of its town of origin, Dzitbalché, Campeche, and probably a copy made in the 18th century. The pages are about the size of those in this book and the cover reads: *The Book of the Dances of the Ancient Men That Were Customary in the Towns at a Time When the White Man Had Not Yet Arrived.* Thus we have an idea of what the Maya sang as they danced, but of the music there is no trace.

All native texts cited heretofore are in Yucatec Maya but mention must be made of two written in other tongues, Quiché and Cakchiquel: the *Popul Vuh*, the Maya "Bible" quoted several times in this book, and the *Anales of the Cakchiqueles*.

Among a succession of priests, both Spanish and Indian, who dedicated themselves to recording data on the Maya culture, the most important, as we have seen, is Bishop Diego de Landa. His *Relación de las Cosas de Yucatán* (Report on the Things of Yucatán) has been of greater assistance to researchers than any other. After his fanatical destruction of codices and "heathen" objects of worship in Maní, he was recalled to Spain to account for his actions. While staying at the Monastery of San Francisco in Guadalajara, Spain, he wrote his *Relación*. The text came to light in 1864, but it is only a condensed version of the original which so far has escaped discovery. Vindicated, Landa returned to Mérida as Bishop in 1573, dying there in 1579. His work provides clues that have made possible the partial deciphering of Maya hieroglyphics.

Franciscan Friar Diego López de Cogolludo's work *Historia de Yucatán* (1688), a compilation and personal interpretation of much earlier eyewitness accounts, provides important source material

Additional information is to be found in the *Relaciones* prepared by Spanish landholders, 1579-81, in answer to a lengthy questionnaire about the Indian culture. This "census" form, to which the Spanish Crown required an answer, was an attempt to gather more information about its colonies and their native inhabitants.

Of interest, too, are the minutes of Inquisition trials held in the 16th century, published by France V. Scholes and Eleanor B. Adams under the title of *Don Diego Quijada, Alcalde Mayor de Yucatán, 1561–1563.*

Aside from the works of authors cited in the text, we fortunately have the *Relación* of Tomás López Medel, written in 1612, on file in the Madrid Academy of History; the *Relación* of Gaspar Antonio Chi (1582), discovered by Scholes in the Archives of the Indies, Seville; the *Historia de Yucatán* (1633) by Bernardo de Lizana; the *Historia de la Provincia de San Vicente de Chiapa y Guatemala de la Orden de Predicadores* (1698) by Francisco Ximénez; and the *Historia de Guatemala o Recordación Florida*, written in the 18th century by Francisco Antonio de Fuentes y Guzmán.

This list is brief and incomplete. The archives in Spain and America contain a wealth of information, some known and some yet to be discovered.

Esta cuarta edicion de THE MAYA WORLD por Demetrio Sodi Morales se terminó de imprimir el 20 de diciembre de1997 en los talleres de Editora Emahaia, S.A. de C.V., Sor Juana I. de la Cruz 301, 50090, **Toluca,** Edo. de México, constando de 1,000 ejemplares.